ADK 6556

A New Owner's
Guide to
COLLIES

JG-151

Overleaf: A Collie adult and puppy photographed by Isabelle Francais.

Opposite page: A Rough Collie owned by Roane Govich.

The Publisher wishes to acknowledge the following owners of the dogs in this book: Karen Barel, Lois and Rob Baylor, Joyce Beddow, Duncan and Libby Beiler, John Buddie, Heather Burns, Gail Byers, Leslie Canavan, Candray Kennels, Daniel Cardoza, Charlotte Coviak, Mary Cox, K. A. deGruchy, Pamela Durazzano, Ruth and Walter Ecker, Ann Marie Ely, Pattie and Jerry Fitzgerald, Mara Foy, Dave Harris, Frank Holmes, Holmhaven Collies, Kim Hundley, Angela Hungerbuhler, Diane Kissal, Joe Koehler, Leann Leer, Bob Mallann, Marguerite McGrath, Carol Medvesky, Dr. Sally Mobraaten, Rebecca Myers, Marlene and Ewing Nicholson, Kimberley Perrelli, Joesph Reno, Sally Richardson, Lily Sayre, Larry Stevick, Ed and Alice Surowiec, Lori Tackabury, Bernice Terry, Laura Van Embden, Kathy Warner, Bob and Doris Werdermann, Diane Wisney, Alice Wharton.

Photographers: Libby Beiler, Richard Beauchamp, Mary Cox, Tara Darling, Isabelle Francais, Forrest Leer, Marguerite McGrath, Robert Pearcy, Vince Serbin, Karen Taylor, Alice Wharton.

The author acknowledges the contribution of Judy Iby for the following chapters: Sport of Purebred Dogs, Identification and Finding the Lost Dog, Traveling with Your Dog, Behavior and Canine Communication, and Health Care.

t.f.h.

Distributed in the UNITED STATES to the Pet Trade by T.F.H. Publications, Inc., One T.F.H. Plaza, Neptune City, NJ 07753; on the Internet at www.tfh.com; in CANADA Rolf C. Hagen Inc., 3225 Sartelon St. Laurent-Montreal Quebec H4R 1E8; Pet Trade by H & L Pet Supplies Inc., 27 Kingston Crescent, Kitchener, Ontario N2B 2T6; in ENGLAND by T.F.H. Publications, PO Box 15, Waterlooville PO7 6BQ; in AUSTRALIA AND THE SOUTH PACIFIC by T.F.H. (Australia), Pty. Ltd., Box 149, Brookvale 2100 N.S.W., Australia; in NEW ZEALAND by Brooklands Aquarium Ltd. 5 McGiven Drive, New Plymouth, RD1 New Zealand; in SOUTH AFRICA, Rolf C. Hagen S.A. (PTY.) LTD. P.O. Box 201199, Durban North 4016, South Africa; in Japan by T.F.H. Publications, Japan—Jiro Tsuda, 10-12-3 Ohjidai, Sakura, Chiba 285, Japan. Published by T.F.H. Publications, Inc.

MANUFACTURED IN THE
UNITED STATES OF AMERICA
BY T.F.H. PUBLICATIONS, INC.

A NEW OWNER'S
GUIDE TO
COLLIES

ALICE WHARTON

Contents

1998 Edition

The Collie is the ideal family dog and playmates for any child.

The versatile Collie still retains his natural herding instincts.

036.7374
WHA

An adorable Collie puppy is hard to resist!

The Collie's athleticism and eagerness to please makes him extremely trainable.

A Collie's greatest love is for his family.

HISTORY and Origin of the Collie

Whether a dog breed is one of the diminutive toys or a giant among the working breeds, all dogs trace their origin to a common ancestor—the one we know today as *Canis lupis*, the wolf. The wolf's transition from creature of the forest to mankind's greatest friend and companion did not happen overnight. It began somewhere in the Mesolithic period, over 10,000 years ago. At that time, just providing food for self and family and staying out of harm's way was undoubtedly the major concern in life. This in itself was no mean feat, considering that the use of tools was extremely limited at this stage of human development.

For centuries, the Collie has been serving man as both a herding and companion dog.

There is little doubt that the observation of the wolf could easily have taught man some effective hunting techniques, and many of the wolf's social habits must have seemed strikingly familiar as well. Wolves found a source of easily secured food in man's discards. The association grew from there.

As the relationship developed through the ages, certain descendants of these increasingly domesticated wolves could be advantageously selected to assist in hunting and other survival pursuits. The wolves that performed any function that lightened early human existence were cherished and allowed to breed, while those that were not helpful or whose temperament proved incompatible were driven away.

These wolves-cum-dogs were not only capable of deciding what game was most apt to be easy prey, they knew how to separate the chosen animal from the herd and also how to bring it to ground. These abilities did not escape the notice of man.

Richard and Alice Feinnes, in their book, *The Natural History of Dogs*, classify most dogs as having descended from one of four major groups: the Dingo Group, the Greyhound Group, the Mastiff Group and the Northern or Arctic Group.

Each of these groups trace back to separate and distinct branches of the wolf family. It is the Northern or Arctic Group of dogs that we are particularly concerned with here. This group is a direct descendent of the rugged northern wolf (*Canis lupis*). Included in the many breeds of this group are the Arctic-type dogs such as the Alaskan Malamute and the Chow Chow, the Terriers, the Spitz-type dogs, including Schipperkes and Corgis, and the true herding breeds, of which the Collie is one of the most important and influential.

Almost all of the Northern Group, like their undomesticated ancestors, maintained the characteristics that protect them from the harsh environment of the upper European countries. Weather-resistant coats were of the ideal texture to protect the dogs from rain and cold. There was a long coarse outer coat that shed snow and rain and a dense undercoat that insulated against sub-zero temperatures. These coats were especially abundant around the neck and chest, thereby offering double protection for the vital organs.

Well-coated tails could cover and protect the nose and mouth if the animal were forced to sleep in the snow. Small ears were not as easily frostbitten or frozen as the large and pendulous ears of some of the other breeds. The muzzle had sufficient length to warm the frigid air before it reached the lungs. Leg length was sufficient to keep the chest and abdomen above the snow line. Tails were carried horizontally or up over the back, rather than trailing behind in the snow.

This is not to indicate that there were no cross breedings of the types, nor that abilities peculiar to one group may not have also have been possessed by another. In fact, some historians believe that many of the Northern dogs that retain a degree of hunting ability owe this strength to their Asian Dingo heritage, which is absent from other breeds whose ancestors were not exposed to this admixture. It is also believed that this cross provided some of these Northern breeds with a more refined attitude and tractability.

With the passing of time, humans realized they could manipulate breedings of these evolving wolves so that the resulting offspring became even more proficient in particular areas. While human populations developed a more sophisticated lifestyle, they also thought up new ways in which the domesticated wolves could be of assistance.

The difference in size provided a more agile dog, and the white markings on the dogs' moving parts were particularly useful in a land where daylight hours were short and night work was not uncommon.

These workers of the flocks had no specific name, or at least none found its way into print until 1617 when first mention of these "collie dogs" is found in describing the habits of a Scottish bishop.

The name Collie actually has several explanations—the word "coalley" meaning black; the Welsh "coelius" meaning faithful or perhaps referring to the Scottish black-faced variety of sheep known as the "colley."

The Collie is an extremely versatile breed. Ch. Bdgaters Katie of Sumerset is not only a conformation and obedience champion, she also competes in draft dog events.

HORSES FOR COURSES

In order to understand the diversity of the British Collie dogs in general and the Collie breed in particular, mention should be made here of a formula once used by British stockmen. These gifted men developed prize livestock guided

by an old adage that stated simply, "Horses for courses." That is, one should choose a formula that will produce a horse best suited to the terrain on which the horse will work. This formula was applied to breeding of all animals, including dogs, and from it came some of the world's most outstanding livestock dogs.

Scotland's old Highland Collie was a large strong dog with an aggressive temperament, ideally suited to controlling the wild highland sheep and untamed highland cattle. The Welsh Collie, another ancestor figuring into the makeup of the modern Collie, was small and agile, perfect for herding flocks of small goats and sheep in the sparsely-populated mountainous region of Wales.

The Welsh Collie was far more an "all-around" type of dog with a distinctly more amiable attitude. He was used for a variety of jobs, such as gathering sheep, driving cattle, and guarding property. Above all, the dogs were very interactive with people and highly domesticated.

The Collie has come a long way, but still does dual duty as both a valuable working dog and a beloved family member.

Some dogs were bred to cover over 100 miles of hilly terrain in a day, subduing large wild ewes. Others were bred for less intensive drive and energy. These working dogs were for the most part somewhat unsound and unattractive by show standards with little appeal to those who wished to

breed dogs for exhibition. Attempts were made to enhance the look of the dogs by Irish Setter and Labrador Retriever crosses, the only alien admixture of which there is positive evidence.

Scottish stockmen discovered these dogs on their way to the great Birmingham, England, market and used them liberally as a cross with their own sheepdogs. The resulting litters contained coats of all lengths. The shorter-coated dogs were bred back to a group of ancestral dogs called the bandog and it was said this combination produced the smooth-coated Collie of today.

Early in the 19th century, the Irish Setter cross was of great importance in the development of the Collie. It drastically altered the predominant black and white color of the breed and is the only possible way, students of genetics tell us, that the Collie color eventually called "sable" could have come about so abruptly. The Setter cross helped to make the Collie taller, heavier, and straighter in leg. It also helped to fill the Collie muzzle.

An athletic dog, the Collie thrives with plenty of activity and exercise. Smooth Collie Inaglen California Raisin, CDX, OA owned by Charlotte Coviak competes in agility.

THE MODERN COLLIE STEPS FORTH

The first recorded Sheepdog trial was held in Wales in 1873. The event was won by a Scottish-bred Collie-type dog named Tweed. The description rendered was of an agile and compact tricolored dog. In addition to having won the herding trial, Tweed was awarded the day's prize of beauty.

Collies were shown in classes made up of the many types of herding dogs and simply classified as Sheepdogs at dog shows of the time. In 1870, however, at a dog show held at the Crystal Palace in London, classes were offered for Sheepdogs Rough and Sheepdogs Smooth. This was one of the first attempts at classifying the Sheepdogs.

Queen Victoria saw several Collies working the flocks at Balmoral Castle and become entranced with them. She brought one back to her kennels, and it was not long before the breed caught on with the fashionable element of Great Britain's wealthier class. Now the Collie was not only a respected working dog, but he was rapidly becoming a fashion statement.

In 1873, a dog named Trefoil was born in the kennels of Mr. S. E. Shirley, one of The Kennel Club of England's founding members. The dog was black, white, and tan, a tricolor, and he was blessed with a magnificent coat. He became the standard of perfection and was heavily used at stud. Trefoil produced a son by the name of Ch. Charlemagne and between them, they created a stud force from which every winning Collie in England descended.

The Collie Club in England was organized in 1881. Classes were offered at the club's shows for both rough and smooth Collies, but The Kennel Club of England did not offer these separate classes until 1895. The standard of excellence was the same for both classifications, aside from coat.

THE COLLIE IN THE UNITED STATES

The earliest stud book of the American Kennel Club (1878)

The agile and intelligent Collie is one of the most trainable breeds in existence. Katie owned by Kathy Warner and Dave Harris shows the fruits of her labors.

contained no Collie listings. However, Volume II of the Stud Book, published in 1885, contained 22 Collies, 19 of which were bred in the United States.

The Collie Club of America was organized in 1886, and it has functioned ever since that time as the parent club for the breed. By the turn of the century, Collies had also gained significant popularity in America. Although generally uneven in type, the breed was developing and improving on both sides of the Atlantic, moving away from the heavier boned and thicker-headed dogs used to maintain the flocks.

In the early 1900s, the breed was fortunate to attract the interest of American fanciers who were not only clever breeders, but who had the financial where-with-all to be able to purchase the stock they needed and campaign it advantageously. Names such as J. Pierpont Morgan, (Cragston Collies), Samuel Untermeyer (Greystone Collies), Mrs. Clara May Lunt of Alstead Kennels, Dr. O. P. Bennett of the Tazewell Kennels, Chris Casselman of Hertzville, Edwin Pickhardt of Sterling, and Willard R.VanDyck of Honeybrook established kennels that were to beneficially influence the breed for decades.

The loyal and sociable Collie's greatest love is for his family.

The next wave of interest developed in the 1920s and 30s and again the breed was blessed with a good number of breeders who were affluent and genuinely influential. The financial status of the breed's support system assisted the breed in surviving America's great depression of the 1930s.

In 1928, Laund Loyalty of Bellhaven was born in England. He was exported to Mrs. Florence B. Ilch in Red Bank, New Jersey. Loyalty was shown only once in his entire life. The show was the Westminster Kennel Club event of 1929 at which he went all the way to Best in Show—the only Collie that has ever done so in the show's history. The Westminster win was followed by threats on Loyalty's life and Mrs. Ilch decided never to show him again.

The Second World War brought a halt to importing dogs from England. America, however, had created its own superb

15

nucleus of breeding stock by then and the breed moved forward, better than it had prior to the war years. This period also saw the rise to prominence of a number of much smaller breeders throughout the country who, though far more limited in scope, contributed significantly to the progress of the breed. The breed began to shift into the hands of these more modest breeders without any pause in its progress or popularity. In fact, breeding done during this financially devastating period of American history paved the way for some of the great Collies bred and campaigned in the 1940s.

One of these individuals was Mrs. William H. Long, Jr. of Oyster Bay, New York. Mrs. Long thought of her Noranda Collies as working dogs and was founder of *Dogs for Defense* during World War II. She also helped to found Buddies, Inc., an organization that provided obedience-trained companion dogs for children who were either blind or handicapped. It is said that her ultimate goal for the Collie was to have "all good Collies with an obedience title."

One of the significant figures in American Collie history was Albert Payson Terhune. He combined his reputation and talent as a writer with his love of Collies by writing books and articles numbering in the hundreds. His stories all had dog heroes in them and these canine heroes possessed qualities that were nothing short of human. Occupying the giant's share of the stories were his own Collies.

Rough Collies Nathan and Trevor owned by Kim Hundley show off the breed's magnificent coat.

Terhune also served on the board of directors of the American Kennel Club and his advocacy of the breed on this level, combined with his contributions as an author, served not only to enhance the position of the breed as a show dog but as a dog no family could afford to be without.

Collie breeders have strived to preserve the breed's natural herding instincts and good temperament.

Terhune's Sunnybank stories were written throughout the 1920s and 1930s. In 1940, author Eric Knight wrote *Lassie Come Home,* a book that not only perpetuated the endearing if not exaggerated human qualities of the Collie, it inspired an extremely successful string of motion pictures and a television series that remains in international reruns into this day.

The Collie has gained worldwide recognition through the heroic portrayal of the breed in books, on television, and in the movies.

CHARACTERISTICS of the Collie

There is probably nothing quite so captivating as a puppy. Most are little bundles of fluff with angelic faces. If you haven't fully decided whether or not to add a Collie puppy to your life, a visit to the home or kennel where there is a litter of puppies is probably not the best idea in the world. Anyone even thinking of dog ownership is going to be hard pressed to resist these little charmers.

The person who anticipates owning a Collie should give serious thought to the final decision. All puppies are cuddly and cute—Collie puppies particularly so. There is nothing

The Collie is a superb guardian and ideal family dog. They are natural "baby-sitters" and wonderful playmates for any child.

more seductive than a litter of Collie puppies at play or nestled together sound asleep, one on top of the other. In addition to being cute, Collie puppies are living, breathing, and very mischievous little creatures. Not only that, they are totally dependent upon their human owner for all their needs once they leave their mother and littermates.

Buying a dog, especially a puppy, before someone is absolutely sure they want to make that commitment can be a serious mistake. The prospective dog owner must clearly understand the amount of time and work involved in dog ownership. Failure to understand the extent of commitment dog ownership involves is one of the primary reasons there are so many unwanted canines that are forced to finish their lives in animal shelters.

Young Collies are constantly investigating and exploring their surroundings. Clandara's Capture the Moment shows her curious nature.

Before anyone contemplates the purchase of a dog, there are some very basic conditions that must be considered. One of the first important questions that must be answered is whether or not the person who will ultimately be responsible for the dog's care and well being actually wants a dog. Often, it is the mother of the household who must take on the responsibility of the family dog's day-to-day care. Although the children in the family, perhaps even the father, may be wildly enthusiastic about having a dog, it must be remembered that they are away most of the day at school or work. It is often "mom" who will be taking on yet another responsibility as primary caregiver for the family dog. Somehow this seems to be the case even where there is a working mom in the family. In addition to her work away from home, there are all those household chores it appears only a mom can handle. Does she, in fact, share the enthusiasm for what could easily become another responsibility on her unending list?

Pets are a wonderful method of teaching children responsibility, but it should

Collie ownership is a big responsibility. Make sure the decision to own one is carefully considered.

Collies are rugged dogs that love being in the great outdoors. Smooth Collie "Sophie" contemplates taking a dip.

be remembered that the enthusiasm that inspires children to promise anything in order to have a new puppy may quickly wane. Who will take care of the puppy once the novelty wears off? Does that person want a dog?

Desire to own a dog aside, does the lifestyle of the family actually provide for responsible dog ownership? If the entire family is away from early morning to late at night, who will provide for all of a puppy's needs? Feeding, exercise, outdoor access, and the like cannot be provided if no one is home. Another important factor to consider is whether or not the breed of dog is suitable for the person or the family with which it will be living. A fully grown Collie can handle the rough and tumble play of young children. A very young Collie puppy may have difficulty in doing so.

Then, too, there is the matter of hair. A luxuriously-coated dog is certainly beautiful to behold, but all that hair takes a great deal of care. To upkeep an adult Collie requires time and patience, to say nothing of some elbow grease. As great as claims are for a Collie's adaptability and intelligence, remember the new dog must be taught every household rule that he is to observe. Some dogs catch on more quickly than others and puppies are just as inclined to forget or disregard lessons as young human children are.

CASE FOR THE PUREBRED DOG

As previously mentioned, all puppies are cute with their little pink tongues and wagging tails. Not all puppies grow up to be particularly attractive adults. What is considered beauty by one person is not necessarily seen as attractive by another. It is almost impossible to determine what a mixed breed puppy will look like as an adult. Nor will it be possible to determine if the mixed breed puppy's temperament is suitable for the person or family who wishes to own him. If the puppy grows up to be too big, too hairy, or too active for the owner, what then will happen to him?

Size and temperament can vary to a degree even within purebred dogs. Still, selective breeding over many generations has produced dogs giving the would-be owner reasonable assurance of what the purebred puppy will look and act like as an adult. Esthetics completely aside, this predictability is more important than one might think.

Purebred puppies will grow up to look like their adult relatives and, by and large, they will behave pretty much like the rest of their family too. Any dog, mixed breed or not, has the potential to be a loving companion;

In terms of grooming, the Rough Collie needs more maintenance than the Smooth. The time you want to spend on grooming should be a consideration when choosing a breed.

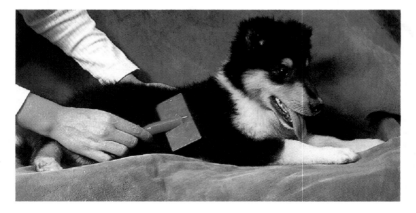

however, the predictability of a purebred dog offers reasonable insurance that he will not only suit the person's esthetic demands, but also the owner's lifestyle as well.

Before you bring a Collie puppy into your household, visit breeders and spend as much time with both puppies and adults as you can. Be sure that the adult Collie is the dog that appeals to you esthetically and temperamentally.

The Collie loves to be with his family and can accompany his owners on any outing. Nine-week-old "Chloe" takes her first trip to the beach.

CHARACTER AND PERSONALITY

The Collie is a gentle devoted companion. The breed learns quickly and is easily trained, but a soft touch is absolutely necessary. Harsh methods are never necessary with this breed and employing a heavy hand could easily destroy the dog's spirit.

A true "dog's dog," Collies love canine companionship and can amuse themselves for hours. A group of Clandara Collies owned by Marguerite McGrath at play.

With their high degree of intelligence, Collies can become bored easily. As a rule they are not a breed that can be left on their own continuously or be kept outdoors alone. Their long-standing history of living and working with man have made them "people dogs." Denied the opportunity to be with those they love, Collies can demand attention by becoming barkers. One of the Collie's finest qualities is his desire to bond with and please his master. Not being allowed to do so can make even the best Collie difficult to live with.

Because of his intelligence and eagerness to please, there are few limits to what the Collie can accomplish. Holmhaven Jason of Sealoch proudly poses with his awards.

The Collie is an ideal family dog in that he is able to share his devotion with every member of the family and has an innate ability to adjust his own mood to that of the family member he is with. He will sound the alarm to alert the family of the approach of a stranger, but will be delighted to greet that same stranger if given assurance that all is well.

TRAINABILITY

As long as a gentle hand is used to train the Collie, there are few limits to what the breed can be trained to do. The modern Collie is just as apt to keep track of the children in a family and guide them away from danger as the Collie of old was required to do with the animals put in his charge generations ago.

The breed's need to be with his owner is most certainly a holdover from the time when there would have been little purpose to a dog that would abandon his flock or the shepherd who shared the responsibility for the flock with the dog.

What so many people find surprising about the Collie is how he can spend his entire life as a docile and loving companion and then rush to the defense of his loved ones with the courage of a lion when faced with danger. All the basics for a marvelous friend and household guardian exist within the framework of the tiniest Collie puppy. It is entirely up to the Collie puppy's owner to bring those characteristics into full bloom.

STANDARD for the Collie

The standard of the Collie is written in a straightforward manner that can be read and understood by even the beginning fancier. The ability to interpret all of its nuances, however, may take many years of experience and observation. Reading as much as possible helps a great deal, but nothing benefits the novice more than putting his or her self in the hands of a dedicated and experienced breeder.

THE OFFICIAL STANDARD FOR THE COLLIE

ROUGH

General Character—The Collie is a lithe, strong, responsive, active dog, carrying no useless timber, standing naturally straight and firm. The deep, moderately wide chest shows strength, the sloping shoulders and well-bent hocks indicate speed and grace, and the face shows high intelligence. The Collie presents an impressive, proud picture of true balance, each part being in harmonious proportion to every other part and to the whole. Except for the technical description that is essential to this Standard and without which no Standard for the guidance of breeders and judges is adequate, it could be stated simply that no part of the Collie ever seems to be out of proportion to any other part. Timidity, frailness, sullenness, viciousness, lack of animation, cumbersome appearance and lack of over-all balance impair the general character.

Head—The head properties are of great importance. When considered in proportion to the size of the dog the head is inclined to lightness and never appears massive. A heavy-headed dog appears lacks the necessary bright, alert, full-of-sense look that

Ch. Websterhill Sunshine Jewel, CDX, HT, HIC, CGC, VC owned by Ann Marie Ely is a perfect example of a well-rounded Collie.

Ch. Tedjoi D'Artagnan owned by Duncan and Libby Beiler has won Best Smooth Collie three times at the famed Westminster Kennel Club in New York City.

contributes so greatly to expression. Both in front and profile view the head bears a general resemblance to a well-blunted lean wedge, being smooth and clean in outline and nicely balanced in proportion. On the sides it tapers gradually and smoothly from the ears to the end of the black nose, without being flared out in backskull and the top of the muzzle lie in two approximately parallel, straight planes of equal length, divided by a very slight but perceptible stop or break. A mid-point between the inside corners of the eyes (which is the center of a correctly placed stop) is the center of balance in length of head.

The end of the smooth, well-rounded muzzle is blunt but not square. The underjaw is strong, clean-cut and the depth of skull from the brow to the under part of the jaw is not excessive. The teeth are of good size, meeting in a scissors bite. *Overshot or undershot jaws are undesirable, the latter being more severely penalized.* There is a very slight prominence of the eyebrows. The backskull is flat, without receding either laterally or backward and the occipital bone is

not highly peaked. The proper width of backskull necessarily depends upon the combined length of skull and muzzle and the width of the backskull is less than its length. Thus the correct width varies with the individual and is dependent upon the extent to which it is supported by length of muzzle. Because of the importance of the head characteristics, *prominent head faults are very severely penalized.*

Eyes—Because of the combination of the flat skull, the arched eyebrows, the slight stop and the rounded muzzle, the foreface must be chiseled to form a receptacle for the eyes and they are necessarily placed obliquely to give them the required forward outlook. Except for the blue merles, they are required to be matched in color. They are almond-shaped, of medium size and never properly appear to be large and prominent. The color is dark and the eye color does not show a yellow ring or a sufficiently prominent haw to affect the dog's expression. The eyes have a clear, bright appearance, expressing intelligent inquisitiveness, particularly when the ears are drawn up and the dog is on the alert. In blue merles, dark brown eyes are preferable, but either or both eyes may be merle or china in color without specific penalty. A large, round, full eye seriously detracts from the desired "sweet" expression. *Eye faults are heavily penalized.*

The Collie puppy is a miniature version of the adult.

Ears—The ears are in proportion to the size of the head and, if they are carried properly and unquestionably "break" naturally, are seldom too small. Large ears usually cannot be lifted, they will be out of proportion to the size of the head. When in repose the ears are folded lengthwise and thrown back into the frill. On the alert they are drawn well up on the backskull and are carried about three-quarters erect, with about one-forth of the ear tipping or "breaking" forward. *A dog with prick ears or low ears cannot show true expression and is penalized accordingly.*

The head is what gives the Collie his distinctive appearance. It should be inclined towards lightness and never massive or coarse looking.

Neck—The neck is firm, clean, muscular, sinewy and heavily frilled. It is fairly long, carried upright with a slight arch at the nape and imparts a proud, upstanding appearance showing off the frill.

Body—The body is firm, hard and muscular, a trifle long in proportion to height. The ribs are well-rounded behind the well-sloped shoulders and the chest is deep, extending to the elbows. The back is strong and level, supported by powerful hips and thighs and the croup is sloped to give a well-rounded finish. The loin is powerful and slightly arched. *Noticeably fat dogs, or dogs in poor flesh, or with skin disease, or with no undercoat are out of condition and are moderately penalized accordingly.*

Legs—The forelegs are straight and muscular, with a fair amount of bone considering the size of the dog. A cumbersome appearance is undesirable. *Both narrow and wide placement are penalized.* The forearm is moderately fleshy and the pasterns are flexible but without weakness. The hind legs are less fleshy, muscular at the thighs, very sinewy and the hocks and stifles are well bent. *A cowhocked dog or a dog with straight stifles is penalized.* The comparatively small feet are approximately oval in shape. The soles are well padded and tough, and the toes are well arched and close together. When the Collie is not in motion the legs and feet are judged by allowing the dog to come to a natural stop in a standing position so that both the forelegs and the hindlegs are placed well apart, with the feet extending straight forward. Excessive "posing" is undesirable.

Gait—Gait is sound. When the dog is moved at a slow trot toward an observer its straight front legs track comparatively close together at the ground. The front legs are not out at the elbows, do not "crossover," nor does the dog move with a choppy, pacing or rolling gait. When viewed from the rear the hind legs are straight, tracking comparatively close together at the ground. At a moderate trot the hind legs are powerful and propelling. Viewed from the side the reasonably long, "reaching" stride is smooth and even, keeping the back line firm and level.

As the speed of the gait is increased the Collie single tracks, bringing the front legs inward in a straight line from the shoulder toward the center line of the body and the hind legs inward in a straight line from the hip toward the center line of the body. The gait suggests effortless speed combined with the dog's herding heritage, requiring it to be capable of changing its direction of travel almost instantaneously.

Tail—The tail is moderately long, the bone reaching to the hock joint or below. It is carried low when the dog is quiet, the end having an upward twist or "swirl." When gaited or when the dog is excited it is carried gaily but not over the back.

Coat—The well-fitting, proper-textured coat is the crowning glory of the rough variety of Collie. It is not abundant except on the head and legs. The outer coat is straight and harsh to the touch. *A soft, open outer coat or a curly outer coat, regardless of quantity is penalized.* The undercoat, however, is soft, furry and so close together that it is difficult to see the skin when the hair is parted. The coat is very abundant on the main and

Ch. Clandara's Silver Screen owned by Marguerite McGrath has a wonderful, well-marked, blue merle coat.

frill. The face or mask is smooth and well feathered to the back of the pasterns. The hind legs are smooth below the hock joints. Any feathering below the hocks is removed for the show ring. The hair on the tail is very profuse and on the hips it is long and bushy. The texture, quantity and the extent to which the coat "fits the dog" are important points.

Color—The four recognized colors are "Sable and White," "Tri-color," "Blue Merle," and "White." There is no preference among them. The "Sable and White" is predominantly sable (a fawn sable color of varying shades from light gold to dark mahogany) with white markings usually on the chest, neck, legs, feet and the tip of the tail. A blaze may appear on the foreface or backskull or both. The "Tri-color" is predominantly black, carrying white markings as in the "Sable and White" and usually has tan shadings as in the "Tri-color." The "white" is predominantly white, preferably with sable, tri-color or blue merle markings.

Size—Dogs are from 24 to 26 inches at the shoulder and weigh from 60 to 75 pounds. Bitches are from 22 to 24 inches at the shoulder, weighing from 50 to 65 pounds. *An undersize or an oversize Collie is penalized according to the extent to which the dog appears to be undersize or oversize.*

Expression—Expression is one of the most important points in considering the relative value of Collies. *Expression,* like the term "character" is difficult to define in words. It is not a fixed point as in color, weight or height and it is something the uninitiated can properly understand only by optical illustration. In general, however, it may be said to be the

Ch. Clandara's Critical Acclaim, HC, is a striking example of a sable and white Collie. Note the mahogany highlights on the golden background.

maintaining the virtues of a breed and eliminating genetic weaknesses. This process is time consuming and costly. Therefore, responsible Collie breeders protect their investment by providing the utmost in prenatal care for their brood matrons and maximum care and nutrition for the resulting

Responsible and experienced breeders put a great deal of time and effort into raising their puppies and will make sure they go to a good home.

offspring. Once the puppies arrive, the knowledgeable breeder initiates a well-thought-out socialization process.

The socialization process is not one to be overlooked. It is what produces a mentally sound dog that will be able to live with people in harmony. Collie puppies need human contact right from the beginning. It is important that the breeder spend a lot of time with each puppy individually in order to establish the human-canine relationship.

The first question a prospective owner should ask a breeder is "What is the number one characteristic you breed for?" Deal only with those breeders that answer "Good temperament." The buyer should also ask what the breeder does with his or her Collies. This will give some insight on the characteristics for which a breeder selects. No matter that a breeder is attempting to breed outstanding show dogs. The responsible Collie breeder puts compatibility far ahead of any other characteristic. It will also tell the buyer what breeders actually live with their own dogs as pets—this is always a good sign.

The best puppies are born and raised in close proximity with their human family. Puppies kept close to their owner from the very beginning of their lives are imprinted with the scents and sounds of humans. Collie puppies born in a barn or garage and given few opportunities to be with humans seldom achieve their full potential as companions.

The buyer should look for cleanliness in both the dogs and the areas in which the dogs are kept. Cleanliness is the first clue that tells you how much the breeder cares about the dogs he or she owns.

The governing kennel clubs in the different countries of the world maintain lists of local and national Collie clubs and breeders that can lead a prospective dog buyer to responsible breeders of quality stock. Should you not be sure of where to contact a respected breeder in your area, we strongly suggest contacting your local kennel club for recommendations.

There is every possibility a reputable breeder resides in your area who will not only be able to provide the right Collie for you, but who will often have the parents of the puppy on the premises as well. This gives you an opportunity to see first hand what kind of dogs are in the background of the puppy you are considering. Good breeders are not only willing to have you see their dogs, but also to inspect the facility in which the dogs are raised. These breeders will also be able to discuss with you problems that exist in the breed and how they deal with these problems.

Do not be surprised if a concerned breeder asks many questions about you and the environment in

Reputable breeders will screen all Collies for genetic diseases before breeding them. Four-year-old Quincy meets his eight-week-old sister Crystal for the first time.

Puppies need a lot of exercise as well as a lot of rest. These two youngsters take a well-deserved rest.

which your Collie will be raised. Good breeders are just as concerned with the quality of the homes to which their dogs are going as you, the buyer, are in obtaining a sound and healthy dog.

Do not think a good Collie puppy can only come from a large kennel. On the contrary, many of the best breeders raise dogs in their home as a hobby. It is important, however, that you not allow yourself to fall into the hands of an irresponsible "backyard breeder." Backyard breeders separate themselves from the small hobby breeder through their lack of responsibility to bring their breeding stock to its full potential. A hobby breeder's dogs find their way into the show and obedience ring and participate in the many activities in which the Collie excels. Quite simply, a backyard breeder is an individual who simply breeds dogs to sell.

If there are no local breeders in your area, there are legitimate and reliable breeders throughout the country that will appear on the Collie club or national kennel club lists.

These established breeders are accustomed to safely shipping puppies to different states and even different countries. Always check references of these breeders and do not hesitate to ask for documentation of their answers. The breeder will undoubtedly have as many questions for you as you will have for him or her. When you call a far away breeder, call at a reasonable hour and expect to have a lengthy conversation. The amount of money you invest in a satisfying telephone conversation may save you huge veterinary costs and a great deal of unhappiness.

HEALTH CONCERNS

All breeds of dogs have genetic problems that must be paid attention to and just because a male and female do not evidence problems, this does not mean their pedigrees are free of something that might be entirely incapacitating. Again, rely upon recommendations from national kennel clubs or local breed clubs when looking for a breeder, as breed health problems can only be eliminated by thoughtful breeders who are willing to breed selectively and discuss these issues openly. It is important that you ask the breeder you are considering about the following health concerns.

Hip Dysplasia

Hip dysplasia is a degenerative deformity of the hip joint that causes lameness and, in advanced cases, extreme pain.

Eye Problems

Collies can be affected with numerous eye problems. The most frequent of these is Collie eye anomaly. This disease has many forms or grades, ranging from slight pigmentation defects that do not and will not effect the dog's vision, to hemorrhage or bleeding of the eye. The latter is the most drastic form and can only be resolved by removal of the eye itself. Progressive retinal atrophy is a less common but far more serious eye problem in Collies that can cause total blindness by the age of three.

Collie Nose

In this situation, the dog's nose becomes heavily crusted, inflamed, and sensitive, and constant licking makes the nose raw. The condition is an allergic reaction to ultraviolet light in both sunlight and snow.

Worm Treatment

Ivermectin™ is a drug commonly used to successfully treat and/or prevent heartworm in dogs. However, it should never be used on Collies or Shetland Sheepdogs. These breeds have either a congenital sensitivity to the drug or a defect in the blood barrier. Use of the drug can cause damage to the brain and spinal cord. Although not all Collies and Shetland Sheepdogs are effected in this way, the drug should be avoided at all costs by owners of these two breeds.

The puppy you choose should be happy, bright eyed, and healthy looking. Four-month-old Darker Than Amber owned by Gail Byers.

Nowadays, many breeders are also certifying elbows and thyroid function with the Orthopedic Foundation for Animals (OFA). Again, it is important that both the buyer and the seller ask questions. This is not to say that the puppy you buy or his relatives will be afflicted with any of the above, but concerned breeders are well aware of their presence in the breed.

The concerned breeder uses all the information you give to match the right puppy with the right home. Households with boisterous children generally need a puppy that differs from the one appropriate for a sedate single adult. The time you spend in making the right selection ensures you get the right Collie for your lifestyle. If questions are not asked, information is not received. We would be highly suspect of a person who is willing to sell you a Collie with "no questions asked."

RECOGNIZING A HEALTHY PUPPY

Most breeders do not release their puppies until they have been given their "puppy shots." Normally, this is at about seven weeks of age. At this age they will bond extremely well with their new owners and the puppies are entirely weaned.

Nursing puppies receive temporary immunization from their mother. Once weaned, however, a puppy is highly susceptible to many infectious diseases that can be transmitted via the hands and clothing of people. Therefore, it behooves you to make sure your puppy is fully inoculated before he leaves his home environment and to know when any additional inoculations should be given.

Above all, the Collie puppy you buy should be a happy bouncy extrovert. Select the puppy that seems outgoing and ready to trust you. Try sitting down on the floor and give lots of consideration to the one that is anxious to come to you and unties your shoelaces or licks your hand. The worst thing you could possibly do is buy a shy, shrinking-violet puppy or one that appears sick and listless because you feel sorry for him.

Play with the puppies you are considering before choosing one to take home. It's more than likely one will choose you first!

Doing this will undoubtedly lead to heartache and difficulty—to say nothing of the veterinary costs that you may incur in getting the puppy well.

If at all possible, take the puppy you are interested in away from his littermates into another room or another part of the kennel. The smells will remain the same for the puppy so he should still feel secure and maintain his outgoing personality, but it will give you an opportunity to inspect the puppy more closely.

A healthy little Collie puppy will be strong and sturdy to the touch, never bony, or on the other hand, obese and bloated. The coat will be lustrous with no sign of dry or flaky skin. The inside of the puppy's ears should be pink and clean. Dark discharge or a bad odor could indicate ear mites, a sure sign of poor maintenance. The healthy Collie puppy's breath smells

Your puppy may miss the company of his dam and littermates when you first bring him home, so pay extra attention to him during this lonely time.

sweet. The teeth are clean and white and there should never be any malformation of the mouth or jaw. The puppy's eyes should be clear and bright. Eyes that appear runny and irritated indicate serious problems. There should be no sign of discharge from the nose, nor should it ever be crusted or runny. Coughing or diarrhea are danger signals, as are any eruptions on the skin. The coat should be soft and lustrous.

The healthy Collie puppy's front legs should be straight as little posts and his movement light and bouncy. Movement should be free and true and there should never be a limp in the puppy's gait. Of course there is always a chubby clumsy puppy or two in a litter but do not mistake this for unsoundness. If ever you have any doubts, discuss them with the breeder.

Remember, the puppy you choose will be living with you for a long time. Make sure the puppy reacts well to you. Run your fingers along the ground and see if the puppy is willing to play. If the puppy has no interest in you and the only thing he

Clandara's Kaleidoscope is just a few months old but is already looking for fun and adventure.

seems to be interested in is getting back to his littermates, definitely choose another puppy.

MALE OR FEMALE?

If you have decided upon the sex of the puppy you want, stand by your choice and do not have someone change your mind because that is "all that is left." Collies are one breed where there aren't a great number of sex-related differences. Actually the biggest difference is in coat. The mature male Collie's coat is far more luxurious (and therefore requires more care for its upkeep). The male Collie's hair is much longer and much thicker around the neck, shoulders, and chest.

Females have their semiannual heat cycles once they have passed nine or ten months of age. During these heat cycles of approximately 21 days, the female must be confined to avoid soiling her surroundings with the bloody discharge that accompanies estrus. She must also be carefully watched to prevent males from gaining access to her or she will become pregnant.

The way a puppy interacts with his littermates will tell you a lot about his personality. It's easy to see who's "top dog" around here!

Although owners of other breeds find training the male not to "lift his leg" and mark his territory indoors troublesome, most Collie males are not difficult to correct in this respect, nor are they roamers. Collie males seldom go wandering. They are far more interested in staying home to watch over their families.

It should be understood that most sexually related problems can be avoided by having the pet Collie "altered." Spaying the female and neutering the male saves the pet owner all the headaches of either of the sexually related problems without changing the character of the breed. If there is any change at all in the altered Collie it is in making the dog an even more amiable companion. Above all, altering your pet precludes the possibility of adding to the serious pet overpopulation problems that exist worldwide.

SELECTING A SHOW–PROSPECT PUPPY

It should be understood that the most any breeder can offer is an opinion on the "show potential" of a particular puppy. The most promising eight-week-old puppy can grow up to be a mediocre adult. A breeder has no control over this. Any predictions breeders make about a puppy's future are based upon their experience with past litters that have produced winning show dogs. It is obvious that the more successful a breeder has been in producing winning Collies over the years, the broader his or her base of comparison will be.

A puppy's potential as a show dog is determined by how closely he adheres to the demands of the standard of the breed. While most breeders concur there is no such thing as "a sure thing" when it comes to predicting winners, they are also quick to agree that the older a puppy is, the better your chances are of making any predictions at all.

It makes little difference to the owner of a pet if his Collie is poorly marked or if an ear does not stand quite right. Neither would it make a difference if a male pup has only one testicle. These faults do not interfere with a Collie becoming a healthy loving companion. However, these flaws would keep that individual from a winning show career.

When picking a show-prospect puppy, do not be swayed by "cuteness" alone. Adorable as they may be, you must seriously consider each puppy's conformation.

While it certainly behooves the prospective buyer of a show-prospect puppy to be as familiar with the standard of the breed as possible, it is even more important for the buyer to put himself into the hands of a successful and respected breeder of winning Collies. The experienced breeder knows there are certain age-related shortcomings in young Collies that maturity will take care of and other faults that completely eliminate it from consideration as a show prospect. Further, most breeders are delighted to find the right homes for their show-prospect puppies and will be particularly helpful in this respect when they know you plan to show one of their dogs.

The important thing to remember in choosing your first show prospect is "cuteness" may not be consistent with quality. An extroverted puppy in the litter might decide he belongs to you. If you are simply looking for a pet, that is the puppy you should take. However, if you are genuinely interested in showing and breeding your Collie, you must keep your head without disregarding good temperament. Give serious consideration to both what the standard says a

Young "Rob" owned by Ed and Alice Suroweic is going through his gangly teenage period, but still shows great promise as a show dog.

show-type Collie must look like and to the breeder's recommendations.

The complete standard of the breed is presented in this book and its content is what, in the end, determines the show potential of a puppy. When we are selecting a show-quality puppy, all the foregoing regarding soundness and health apply here as well. A point to remember, however, is that spaying and neutering are not reversible procedures and once done, eliminate the possibility of ever breeding or showing your Collie in conformation shows. Altered dogs can, however, be shown in obedience and herding trials and many other competitive events.

There are a good number of additional points to be considered for the show dog as well. When we are selecting a show-quality puppy, we are looking for overall balance and that "look at me attitude" that is so important in the show ring. A show dog is put under a lot more stress than a companion dog that spends his days at home. It is important that the show dog be able to hold up under the stress that will be created by sometimes constant travel. Even in an eight-week-old puppy, we expect to see good movement and soundness that are of paramount importance when judging this working breed. The dogs have to be sturdy but moderate in bone, and above all, agile in order to perform as stock dogs. Though not a great number of show Collies double as stock dogs, there is no reason why they should be any less sound and agile than their working relatives.

PUPPY OR ADULT?

A young puppy is not your only option when contemplating the purchase of a Collie. In some cases, an adult dog or older puppy may be just the answer. It certainly eliminates the trials and tribulations of housebreaking, chewing, and

Proper socialization with littermates is important for a well-adjusted Collie. These two guys seem to get along just fine!

A Collie puppy should be curious about the world around him. Storm owned by Karen Barel takes time out to smell the daffodils.

the myriad of other problems associated with a very young puppy. Inoculations become a once-a-year thing instead of the frequent puppy shots. Very often, the adult Collie will be already spayed or neutered.

Collies are fairly easy to re-home. They love people and, just as long as their new home is one where attention and love abound, an adult Collie will manage to adapt quite well. A few adult Collies may have become set in their ways and while you may not have to contend with the problems of puppyhood, do realize there is the occasional adult that may have developed habits that do not entirely suit you or your lifestyle. Arrange to bring an adult Collie into your home on a trial basis so that neither you nor the dog will be obligated should either of you decide you are incompatible.

IMPORTANT PAPERS

The purchase of any purebred dog entitles you to three very important documents: a health record containing an inoculation list, a copy of the dog's pedigree, and the registration certificate.

Health Record

Most Collie breeders have initiated the necessary inoculation series for their puppies by the time they are eight weeks of age. These inoculations protect the puppies against hepatitis, leptospirosis, distemper, and canine parvovirus. In most cases, rabies inoculations are not given until a puppy is four months of age or older.

There is a set series of inoculations developed to combat these infectious diseases and it is extremely important that you obtain a record of the shots your puppy has been given and the dates upon which the shots were administered. In this way, the veterinarian you choose will be able to continue on with the appropriate inoculation series as needed.

Pedigree

The pedigree is your dog's "family tree." The breeder must supply you with a copy of this document authenticating your puppy's ancestors back to at least the third generation. All purebred dogs have a pedigree. The pedigree does

The breeder you purchase your Collie from should run a quality facility and the puppies should be clean and well taken care of.

not imply that a dog is of show quality. It is simply a chronological list of ancestors.

Registration Certificate

The registration certificate is the canine world's "birth certificate." This certificate is issued by a country's governing kennel club. When you transfer the ownership of your Collie from the breeder's name to your own name, the transaction is entered on this certificate. Once this is mailed to the kennel club, it is permanently recorded in their computerized files. Keep all these documents in a safe place as you will need them when you visit your veterinarian or should you ever wish to breed or show your Collie.

DIET INSTRUCTIONS

Happy healthy Collie puppies are that way because the breeder has been carefully feeding and caring for them. Every breeder we know does this in their own particular way. Most breeders give the new owner a written record that details the amount and kind of food a puppy has been receiving. Follow these recommendations to the letter at least for the first month or two after the puppy comes to live with you. The instructions should indicate the number of times a day your puppy has been accustomed to being fed and the kind of vitamin supplementation he has been receiving. Following the prescribed procedure will reduce the chance of upset stomach and loose stools.

Don't let that innocent face fool you! A Collie puppy will need close supervision to keep him safe and out of mischief.

Usually a breeder's instructions project the increases and changes in food that will be necessary as your puppy grows from week to week. If he does not include this information, ask him for suggestions regarding increases and the eventual changeover to adult food. In the unlikely event you are not informed about the diet by the breeder, your veterinarian will be able to advise you in this respect.

There are countless foods now being manufactured expressly to meet the nutritional needs of puppies and growing dogs. A trip down the pet aisle at your supermarket or pet supply store will prove just how many choices you have. Two important tips to remember: Read labels carefully for content, and when dealing with established reliable manufacturers, remember that you are more likely to get what you pay for.

HEALTH GUARANTEE

Your Collie will look to you, his owner, for the care, discipline, and guidance he needs to become a valued family member.

Any reputable breeder is more than willing to supply a written agreement that the sale of your Collie is contingent upon several things. Although all are equally important, certainly the puppy must be able to pass a veterinarian's examination. Further, the puppy should be guaranteed against the development of any hereditary problems. Last, but not least, the temperament of the puppy you purchase should be vouched for. There is a period of adjustment that all puppies go through when they first go to a new home, but that should be relatively short.

Ideally you will be able to arrange an appointment with your chosen veterinarian right after you have picked up your puppy from the breeder and before you take the puppy home. If this is not possible, you should not delay this procedure any longer than 24 hours from the time you take your puppy home. Take the results of any tests to your veterinarian that the breeder may have had completed on your puppy, such as eye examinations or hearing examinations.

TEMPERAMENT AND SOCIALIZATION

Temperament is both hereditary and learned. Inherited good

temperament can be ruined by poor treatment and lack of proper socialization. A Collie puppy that has inherited a

If properly introduced, your Collie will get along famously with other pets.

bad temperament is a risk as a companion, a show dog, or a working dog and should certainly never be bred. It is therefore critical that you obtain a happy puppy from a breeder who is determined to produce good temperaments and has taken all the necessary steps to provide the early socialization necessary.

It is important to remember a Collie puppy may be as happy as a lark living at home with you and your family, but if the socialization begun by the breeder is not continued, that sunny disposition may not extend outside your front door. From the day the young Collie arrives at your home you must be committed to accompanying him upon an unending pilgrimage to meet and like all human beings and animals.

If you are fortunate enough to have children well past the toddler stage in the household or living nearby, your socialization task will be assisted considerably. Collies raised with children seem to have a distinct advantage in socialization. The two seem to understand each other and in some way, known only to the puppies and children themselves, they give each other the confidence to face the trying ordeal of

Interestingly, many Collie owners find two dogs easier to care for than one. These two friends occupy their time with a game of tug-of-war.

growing up. The children in your own household are not the only children your puppy should spend time with. It is a case of the more the merrier! Every child (and adult for that matter) that enters your household should be asked to pet your puppy.

Your puppy should go everywhere with you—the post office, the market, the shopping mall—wherever. Little Collie puppies create a stir wherever they go and dog lovers will want to stop and pet the puppy. There is nothing in the world better for the puppy. They are social dogs by nature.

If your Collie has a show career in his future, there are other things in addition to just being handled that will have to be

Your Collie pup should go everywhere with you. The more people he meets, the better socialized he will become.

taught. All show dogs must learn to have their mouths opened and inspected by the judge. The judge must be able to check the teeth. Males must be accustomed to having their testicles touched as the dog show judge must determine that all male dogs are "complete," which means there are two normal sized testicles in the scrotum. These inspections must begin in puppyhood and done on a regular and continuing basis.

All Collies must learn to get on with other dogs as well as with humans. If you are fortunate enough to have a "puppy preschool" or dog training class nearby, attend with as much regularity as you possibly can. A young Collie that has been exposed regularly to other dogs from puppyhood will learn to adapt and accept other dogs and other breeds much more readily than one that seldom sees strange dogs.

THE ADOLESCENT COLLIE

You will find it amazing how quickly the little ball of fluff you first brought home begins to develop into a full-grown Collie. Some lines shoot up to full size very rapidly, others mature more slowly. Some Collies pass through adolescence quite gracefully, but most grow out of their puppy fluff and become lanky and ungainly—growing in and out of proportion seemingly from one day to the next.

Food needs to increase during this growth period. However, some Collies seem as if they can never get enough to eat while others experience a very finicky stage in their eating habits and seem to eat enough only to keep from starving. Think of Collie puppies as individualistic as children and act accordingly. The amount of food you give your Collie should be adjusted to how much he will readily consume at each meal. If the entire meal is eaten quickly, add a small amount to the next feeding and continue to do so as the need increases. This method will ensure you give your puppy enough food, but you must also pay close attention to the dog's appearance and conditions, as you do not want a Collie of any age to become overweight or obese.

At eight weeks of age, most Collie puppies are accustomed to eating four meals a day. By the time the puppy is four months old, he can do well on two meals a day, fed morning and evening, with perhaps a snack in the middle of the day. If your puppy does not eat the food offered, he is either not hungry or not well. Your dog will eat when he is hungry. If you suspect the dog is not well, a trip to the veterinarian is in order.

After a Collie is one year old, he can be fed once a day just after your own dinner time. In this way, a trip outdoors just before bed time will usually ensure that the dog will spend an accident-free night.

Children and Collies have a special bond and caring for a dog teaches a child responsibility.

Many dog owners feel their dogs need to be fed more food than what they actually require. Overfeeding is very harmful. It puts stress on a dog's kidneys and heart. It can also make a dog very lazy and consequently cause him to gain even more weight from lack of exercise.

Feeding a diet too high in protein can be harmful to the Collie in that it can lead to "hot spots" (eruptions in the skin), particularly in the rough-coated dog. The rough coat keeps the Collie's body well insulated. Protein creates heat and too much leads to skin problems.

An older Collie can be a loving addition to any household. "Julia" owned by Leann Leer dutifully poses for a Christmas picture.

This adolescent period is a particularly important and sometimes difficult one. Hormones are developing and they can have an effect on the temperament of the dog. Males may begin to test their ability to dominate. Females can get giddy and act foolishly.

This is also the time your Collie must learn all the household and social rules that he will live with for the rest of his life. Your patience and commitment during this difficult time will not only produce a respected canine good citizen, but will forge a bond between the two of you that will grow and ripen into a wonderful relationship.

CARING for Your Collie

FEEDING AND NUTRITION

The best way to make sure your Collie puppy is obtaining the right amount and the correct type of food for his age is to follow the diet instructions provided by the breeder from whom you obtained your puppy. Do your best not to change the puppy's diet and you will be less apt to run into digestive problems and diarrhea. Diarrhea is very serious in young puppies. Puppies with diarrhea can dehydrate very rapidly, causing severe problems and even death.

If it is necessary to change your puppy's diet for any reason, it should never be done abruptly. Begin by adding a tablespoon or two of the new food, gradually increasing the amount until the meal consists entirely of the new product. A rule of thumb: You should be able to feel the ribs and backbone of your dog with just a slight layer of fat and muscle over them.

Overfeeding is very harmful to the Collie. It puts stress on the kidneys and heart. It also can make a Collie very lazy and disinterested in the exercise necessary to keep the breed in shape. By the time your Collie puppy is one year old, you can reduce feedings to one a day. This meal can be given either in the morning or evening. It is really a matter of choice on your part. There are two important things to remember: Feed the main meal at the same time everyday and make sure that what you feed is nutritionally complete.

Choose a good-quality dog food for your Collie that is formulated for his stage of life. Puppies need a growth formula.

If you wish, the single meal can be cut in half and fed twice a day. A morning or night time snack of hard dog biscuits made especially for large dogs can also be given. These biscuits not only become highly anticipated treats, but are genuinely helpful in maintaining healthy gums and teeth.

Provide your Collie pup with his necessary nutrients or he may go out and find his own!

"Balanced" Diets

In order for a canine diet to qualify as "complete and balanced" in the United States, it must meet standards set by the Subcommittee on Canine Nutrition of the National Research Council of the National Academy of Sciences. Most commercial foods manufactured for dogs meet these standards and prove this by listing the ingredients contained in the food on every package and can. The ingredients are listed in descending order with the main ingredient listed first.

Fed with any regularity at all, refined sugars can cause your Collie to become obese and will definitely create tooth decay. Refined sugars are not a part of the canine natural food acquisition, and canine teeth are not genetically disposed to handling these sugars. Do not feed your Collie sugar products and avoid products that contain sugar to any high degree.

Fresh water and a properly prepared balanced diet containing the essential nutrients in correct proportions are all a healthy Collie needs to have offered to him. Dog foods come canned, dry, semi-moist, "scientifically fortified," and "all-natural." A visit to your local supermarket or pet store will reveal how vast an array from which you can select.

The important thing to remember is that all dogs are carnivorous (meat-eating) animals. While the vegetable content of your dog's diet should not be overlooked, a dog's physiology and anatomy are based upon carnivorous food acquisition.

Animal protein and fats are essential to the well being of your Collie. However, a diet too high in proteins can lead to problems as well. Not all dry foods contain the proper amount of protein that will keep the healthy Collie in top condition. It is best to discuss this with the breeder from whom you purchase your dog or with your veterinarian.

It should also be realized that in the wild, carnivores eat practically the entire beast they capture and kill. The carnivore's kills consist almost entirely of herbivore (plant eating) animals and invariably the carnivore begins his meal with the contents of the herbivore's stomach. This provides the carbohydrates, minerals, and nutrients present in vegetables.

Through centuries of domestication we have made our dogs entirely dependent upon us for their well being. Therefore we, as owners, are completely responsible for duplicating the food balance the wild dog finds in nature. The domesticated dog's diet must include protein, carbohydrates, fats, roughage, and small amounts of essential minerals and vitamins.

Finding commercially-prepared diets that contain all the necessary nutrients will not present a problem. It is important to understand though that these commercially-prepared foods do contain all the necessary nutrients your Collie needs. It is therefore unnecessary to add vitamin supplements to these

The POPup™ is a healthy treat for your Collie. Its bone-hard structure helps control plaque and when microwaved, it becomes a rich cracker that your Collie will love. It is available in different flavors and is fortified with calcium.

The breeder will have started your Collie on the road to good nutrition, so stick to this original diet when you first bring him home.

diets in other than special circumstances prescribed by your veterinarian. These "special" periods in a Collie's life can include the time of rapid growth the breed experiences in puppyhood, the female's pregnancy, and the time during which she is nursing her puppies. Even when required in these special circumstances, it is not a case of "if a little is good, more is better." Oversupplementation and forced growth are now looked upon by some breeders as major contributors to many skeletal abnormalities found in the purebred dogs of the day.

Oversupplementation

A great deal of controversy exists today regarding the orthopedic problems that afflict some Collies and many other breeds. Some claim these problems and a wide variety of chronic skin conditions are entirely hereditary, but many others feel they can be exacerbated by diet and overuse of mineral and vitamin supplements for puppies.

Your Collie puppy's food intake needs to be adjusted during his growth periods. Each puppy is an individual, however, so adjust his diet accordingly.

In giving vitamin supplementation, never exceed the prescribed amount. Some breeders insist all recommended dosages be halved before including them in a dog's diet because of the highly fortified commercial foods being fed. Still, other breeders feel no supplementation should be given at all, believing a balanced diet that includes plenty of milk products and a small amount of bone meal is all that is necessary and beneficial.

If the owner of a Collie normally eats healthy nutritious food, there is no reason why their dog can not be given table scraps. Table scraps, however, should be given only as part of the dog's meal and never from the table. A Collie that becomes accustomed to being hand fed from the table very quickly can become a real pest at meal time. Also, dinner guests may find the pleading stare of your Collie less than appealing when dinner is being served.

Dogs do not care if food looks like a hot dog or wedge of cheese. Truly nutritious dog foods are seldom manufactured to look like food that appeals to humans. Dogs only care about how food smells and tastes. It is highly doubtful you will be eating your dog's food, so do not waste your money on these "looks just like" products.

Along these lines, most of the moist foods or canned foods that have the "delicious red beef" look appear that way

Collies require some vegetable matter in their diet. The Carrot Bone™ by Nylabone® serves the function of plaque control, satisfies the need to chew, and is nutritious. It is highly recommended for your Collie.

because they contain great amounts of preservatives, sugars, and dyes. These additives are no better for your dog than they are for you.

Special Diets

There are now any number of commercially prepared diets for dogs with special dietary needs. The overweight, underweight, or geriatric dog can have his nutritional needs met, as can puppies and growing dogs. The calorie content of these foods is adjusted accordingly. With the correct amount of the right foods and the proper amount of exercise, your Collie should stay in top shape. Common sense must prevail. What works for humans works for dogs as well—increasing calories will increase weight; stepping up exercise and reducing calories will bring weight down.

Occasionally a young Collie going through the teething period will become a finicky eater. The concerned owner's first response is to tempt the dog by hand feeding him special treats and foods that the problem eater seems to prefer. This practice only serves to compound the problem. Once the dog learns to play the waiting game, he will turn up his nose at anything other than his favorite food, knowing full well that what he wants to eat will eventually arrive. Give your Collie the proper food you want him to eat. The dog may well turn up his nose a day or two and refuse to eat anything. However, you can rest assured when your dog is really hungry, he will eat.

Unlike humans, dogs have no suicidal tendencies. A healthy dog will not starve himself to death. He may not eat enough to keep himself in the shape we find ideal and attractive, but he will definitely eat enough to maintain himself. If your Collie is not eating properly and appears to be too thin, it is probably best to consult your veterinarian.

BATHING AND GROOMING

The Collie is a natural breed that requires no clipping or trimming. This does not mean the breed needs no coat care at all. Regular thorough brushing and a bath when needed are an important part of keeping your dog a clean, healthy, and pleasant companion.

Many people think a Collie's coat is hard to manage. This need not be true. The male dog will shed twice a year—once in the summer and once around his birthday. The female will shed just after being in heat and when she has a litter of puppies. If she has been spayed, she will also shed when she would normally have been in heat. Brushing is, of course, very important at this time. The rest of the year, although there will always be a few hairs around, the amount is minimal. The nice thing about the Collie's long hair is that it does not burrow into the sofa or clothing. It can be taken up with your hand with little or no difficulty.

It is not necessary to give your Collie a bath unless he begins to smell foul. You can freshen up the coat by sprinkling a little baby powder into it, working it in well, and then brushing it out. This, of course, also helps to make the dog smell very good. This procedure can even help if the dog has gotten into

substances in his longer furnishings. Should you encounter a mat that does not brush out easily, use your fingers and the steel comb to separate the hairs as much as possible. Do not cut or pull out the matted hair. Apply baby powder or one of the especially prepared grooming powders directly to the mat and brush completely from the skin out.

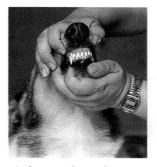

A thorough oral inspection should be a part of your Collie's grooming routine.

Nail Trimming

This is a good time to accustom your Collie to having his nails

Shaving the Collie's coat in the summer is not necessary, as it acts as insulation against the heat as well as the cold.

trimmed and having his feet inspected. Your puppy may not particularly like this part of his toilette, but with patience and time he will eventually resign himself to the fact that these "manicures" are a part of life. Nail trimming must be

done with care because it is important not to cut into the "quick." Dark nails make it difficult to see the quick, which grows close to the end of the nail and contains very sensitive nerve endings. If the nail is allowed to grow too long, it will be impossible to cut it back to a proper length without cutting into the quick. This causes severe pain to the dog and can also result in a great deal of bleeding that can be very difficult to stop.

The nails of a Collie who spends most of his time indoors or on grass when outdoors can grow long very quickly. Do not allow the nails to become overgrown and then expect to cut them back easily. If your Collie is getting plenty of exercise on cement or rough hard pavement, the nails may wear down sufficiently. Otherwise they must be carefully trimmed back.

Should the quick be nipped in the trimming process, there are any number of blood-clotting products available at pet

If you accustom your Collie to grooming procedures when he is young, he will come to think of it as a pleasant experience.

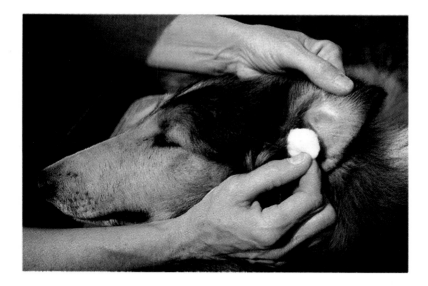

Your Collie's ears must be kept clean and free of waxy build-up. shops that will almost immediately stem the flow of blood. It is wise to have one of these products on hand in case there is a nail trimming accident or the dog tears a nail on his own.

There are coarse metal files available at your pet emporium or hardware store that can be used in place of the nail clippers. This is a more gradual method of taking the nail back and one that is far less apt to injure the quick.

The Wet Bath

Consistent brushing and a wash cloth will keep the Collie's coat surprisingly clean, however, there are occasions where a full bath may be required. On the occasion your Collie requires a wet bath, you will need to gather the necessary equipment ahead of time. A rubber mat should be placed at the bottom of the tub so the dog can avoid slipping and becoming frightened. A rubber spray hose is absolutely necessary to remove all shampoo residue.

A small cotton ball placed inside each ear will avoid water running down into the dog's ear canal. Be very careful when washing around the eyes as soaps and shampoos can be extremely irritating. A tiny dab of petroleum jelly or a drop of mineral oil in each eye will help prevent shampoo irritating the eye.

In bathing, start behind the ears and work back. Use a wash cloth to soap and rinse around the head and face. Once you have shampooed your dog, you must rinse the coat thoroughly and when you feel quite certain all shampoo residue has been removed, rinse once more. Shampoo residue in the coat is sure to dry the hair and cause skin irritation.

As soon as you have completed the bath, use heavy towels to remove as much of the excess water as possible. Your Collie will undoubtedly assist you in the process by shaking a great deal of the water out of his coat on his own.

Brush drying the coat with the assistance of a hair dryer (human or special canine blower-type) will reduce drying time significantly. When using a hair dryer of any kind, always keep the setting on "medium." Anything warmer can dry the coat and, in extreme cases, actually burn the skin. Do not face the dryer directly into the coat, but go over it, and use your brush to fluff out the hair and assist the drying process.

EXERCISE

Sufficient exercise is just good sense. Remember the breed's heritage—the Collie was bred to work a full day, every day!

Needless to say, puppies should never be forced to exercise. Normally they are little dynamos of energy and keep themselves busy all day long, taking frequent naps.

Mature Collies are not only capable of running distances, but are delighted to be jogging companions. It is important, however, to use good judgment in any exercise program. Begin slowly and increase the distance to be covered very gradually over an extended period of time. Use special precautions in hot weather. High temperatures and forced exercise are a dangerous combination.

The best exercise for a Collie is the kind he acquires in the

A Collie that competes in conformation must become accustomed to extensive grooming.

Provide your Collie with adequate shelter from the elements if he is to be kept outside for long periods of time.

pursuit of the many organized activities for which the breed is particularly well suited. Agility, flyball, obedience, and herding activities exercise the Collie's mind and his body. There is no better way to ensure your Collie of a happy healthy existence.

SOCIALIZATION

It should be understood that a young dog that has never been exposed to strangers, traffic noises, or boisterous children could become confused and frightened. It is important that a Collie owner give his or her dog the opportunity to experience all of these situations gradually and with his trusted owner present for support. Collies are good-natured happy dogs in general and very pleasant to be around. They are social dogs by nature, but a dog that is never given the opportunity to experience new and different things will grow to be quite hesitant about life in general. Do help your Collie to develop the wonderful loving personality that is his heritage.

HOUSEBREAKING and Training Your Collie

There is no breed of dog that cannot be trained. It does appear, however, that some breeds are more difficult to get the desired response from than others. In many cases, however, this has more to do with the trainer and his or her training methods than it does with the dog's inability to learn. With the proper approach, any dog can be taught to be a good canine citizen. Many dog owners do not understand how a dog learns, nor do they realize they can be breed specific in their approach to training.

Collies are extremely sensitive animals. Whereas it may be necessary to employ stern measures just to get the attention of some breeds, a Collie will be shattered by a scolding. The breed lives to please, and all an owner needs to do is let the mischievous Collie know he has misbehaved and you will have a dejected little fellow on your hands.

Young Collie puppies have an amazing capacity to learn. This capacity is greater than most humans realize. It is important to remember that these young puppies also forget with great speed unless they are reminded of what they have learned by continual reinforcement.

As Collie puppies leave the nest, they began their search for two things: a pack leader and the rules set down by that leader that the puppies can follow. Too many owners fail miserably in supplying these very basic needs. Instead, the owner immediately begins to respond to the demands of the puppy, and this can lead to a very confused and demanding youngster. For example, a Collie puppy quickly learns he will be allowed into the house because he is whining, not because he can only enter the house when he is not whining. Instead of learning the only way he will be fed is to follow a set procedure, i.e., sitting or lying down on command, the poorly educated Collie puppy learns that leaping about the kitchen, barking up a storm, and creating a stir is the behavior that gets results.

The key to successful training lies in establishing the proper relationship between dog and owner. The owner or the owning family must be the pack leader and the individual or family must provide the rules by which the dog abides. Once this is established, a Collie will live to be praised by his pack leader.

The Collie is easily trained to do almost any task. It is important to remember, however, that the breed does not comprehend violent treatment. A Collie's spirit can break very quickly and easily by heavy-handed treatment. Patient positive reinforcement is the key to successfully training a Collie. Always show your dog the right thing to do and be consistent in having him behave that way.

HOUSEBREAKING

The method of housebreaking we recommend is the avoidance of accidents. We take a puppy outdoors to relieve himself after every meal, after every nap, and after every 15 or 20 minutes of playtime. We carry the puppy outdoors to avoid the opportunity of an accident occurring on the way.

Housebreaking your Collie becomes a much easier task with the use of a crate. Most breeders use the fiberglass-type crates approved by the airlines for shipping live animals. They are easy to clean and can be used for the entire life of the dog.

A crate provides your Collie with a safe place to retreat and call his own.

Some first-time dog owners may see the crate method of housebreaking as cruel. What they do not understand is that all dogs need a place of their own to retreat. A puppy will soon look to his crate as his own private den. Use of a crate reduces housetraining time down to an absolute minimum and avoids keeping a puppy under constant stress by incessantly correcting him for making mistakes in the house. The anti-crate advocates who consider it cruel to confine a puppy for any length of time do not seem to have a problem with constantly harassing and punishing the puppy because he has wet on the carpet and relieved himself behind the sofa.

Begin using the crate when you feed your Collie puppy. Keep the door closed and latched while the puppy is eating. When the meal is finished, open the crate and carry the puppy outdoors to

If you take your Collie pup outside to the same place to eliminate, he will soon know what is expected of him.

the spot where you want him to learn to eliminate. In the event you do not have outdoor access or will be away from home for long periods of time, begin housebreaking by placing newspapers in some out of the way corner that is easily accessible for the puppy. If you consistently take your puppy to the same spot, you will reinforce the habit of going there for that purpose.

Block off an area for your Collies to play in when you cannot supervise them. Your puppies, and your belongings, will be much safer.

As your Collie puppy grows, you will undoubtedly want to train him to eliminate outdoors and, in many cases, the dog will prefer to do so. This can be accomplished very simply by getting the paper-trained puppy outdoors immediately after eating. Lavish praise after the puppy has eliminated will most often get the message across.

In any case, it is important that you do not let the puppy loose after eating. Young puppies will eliminate almost immediately after eating or drinking. They will also be ready to relieve themselves when they first wake up and after playing. If you keep a watchful eye on your puppy, you will quickly learn when this is about to take place. A puppy usually circles and sniffs the floor just before he will relieve himself. Do not give your puppy an opportunity to learn that he can eliminate in the house or away from his designated spot! Your housetraining chores will be reduced considerably if you avoid bad habits in the first place.

If you are not able to watch your puppy every minute, he should be in his crate with the door securely latched. Each time you put your puppy in the crate, give him a small treat of some kind. Throw the treat to the back of the crate and encourage the puppy to walk in on his own. When he does so, praise the puppy and perhaps hand him another piece of the treat through the wires of the cage.

Understand that a Collie puppy of eight to twelve weeks will not be able to contain himself for long periods of time. Puppies of that age must relieve themselves often except at night. Your schedule must be adjusted accordingly. Also make sure your puppy has relieved himself at night just before the last member of the family retires.

Your first priority in the morning is to get the puppy outdoors. Just how early this will take place will depend much more upon your puppy than upon you. If your Collie puppy is like most others there will be no doubt in your mind when he needs to be let out. You will also learn very quickly to tell the difference between the *Getting your puppy used to his collar and leash is the first step in training your Collie.* puppy's "emergency" signals and just unhappy grumbling. Do not test the young puppy's ability to contain himself. His vocal demand to be let out is confirmation that the housebreaking lesson is being learned.

Naturally, if you find it necessary to be away from home all day, you will not be able to leave your puppy in a crate but, on the other hand, do not make the mistake of allowing him to roam the house or even a large room at will. Confine the puppy to a small room or partitioned-off area and cover the floor with newspaper. Make this area large enough so that the puppy will not have to relieve himself next to his bed, food, or water bowls. You will soon find the puppy will be inclined to use one particular spot to perform his bowel and bladder functions. When you are home you must take the puppy to this exact spot to eliminate at the appropriate time.

BASIC TRAINING

It is important for Collie owners to remember that the breed thrives and grows on learning. The Collie has a great capacity to learn and if his ability is not activated in a positive manner by the dog's owner, the dog can become incredibly creative in ways that may not be entirely pleasing.

Training should never take place when you are irritated, distressed, or preoccupied. Nor should you begin basic training in crowded or noisy places that will interfere with you or your dog's concentration. Once the commands are understood and learned, you can begin testing your dog in public places, but at first the two of you should work in a place

Crate training is the fastest and easiest way to housebreak your Collie.

where you can concentrate fully upon each other

The No Command

There is no doubt whatsoever that one of the most important commands your Collie puppy will ever learn is the meaning of "No!" It is extremely important that your puppy learn this command just as soon as possible. One important piece of advice in using this and all other commands—never give a Collie puppy a command you are not prepared and able to enforce! The only way a puppy learns to obey commands is to realize that once issued, commands must be complied with. Learning the no command should start the first day of the puppy's arrival at your home.

Leash Training

It is never too early to accustom your puppy to his leash and collar. The leash and collar are your fail-safe ways of keeping your dog under control. It may not be necessary for the puppy or adult Collie to wear his collar and identification tags within the confines of your home, but no dog should ever leave home without a collar and without the leash held securely in your hand.

It is best to begin getting your puppy accustomed to his collar by leaving a soft collar around his neck for a few minutes at a time. Gradually extend the time you leave the collar on. Most Collie puppies become accustomed to their collar very quickly and after a few scratches to remove it, forget they are even wearing one.

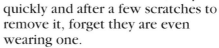

Always keep your Collie on lead when outside to keep him from becoming separated from you.

While you are playing with the puppy, attach a lightweight leash to the collar. Do not try to guide the puppy at first. The point here is to accustom the puppy to the feeling of having something attached to the collar. Encourage your puppy to follow you as you move away. Should the puppy be reluctant to cooperate, coax him along with a treat of some kind. Hold the treat in front of the puppy's nose to encourage him to follow you. Just as soon as the puppy takes a few steps toward you, praise him enthusiastically and continue to do so as you continue to move along.

Make the initial sessions short and fun. Continue the lessons in your home or yard until the puppy is completely unconcerned about the fact that he is on a leash. With a treat in one hand and the leash in the other, you can begin to use both to guide the puppy in the direction you wish to go. Begin your first walks in front of the house and eventually extend them down the street and eventually around the block.

The Come Command

The next most important lesson for the any puppy to learn is to come when called. Therefore it is very important that the puppy learn his name as soon as possible. Constantly repeating the dog's name will do the trick. Use the puppy's name every time you speak to him. "Want to go outside, Lad?" "Come Lad, come!"

Learning to come on command could save your Collie's life when the two of you venture out into the world. Come is the command a dog must understand has to be obeyed without question, but the dog should not associate that command with fear. Your dog's response to his name and the word come should always be associated with a pleasant experience, such as great praise and petting or a food treat.

All too often novice trainers get very angry at their dog for not responding immediately to the come command. When the dog finally does come after a chase, the owner scolds the dog for not obeying. The dog begins to associate "come" with an unpleasant result.

Properly training your puppy will make grooming sessions much more pleasurable. This Collie owned by Lori Tackabury stands still to be brushed.

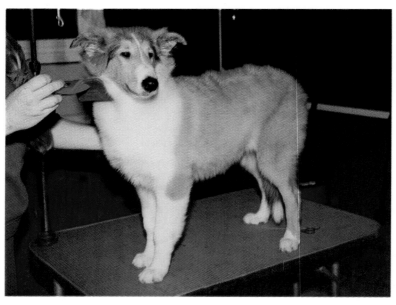

It is much easier to avoid the establishment of bad habits than it is to correct them once set. Avoid at all costs giving the come command unless you are sure your puppy will come to you. The very young puppy is far more inclined to respond to learning the come command than the older dog who will be less dependent upon you.

Use the command initially when the puppy is already on his way to you or give the command while walking or running away from the youngster. Clap your hands and sound very happy and excited about having the puppy join in on this "game."

The very young Collie will normally want to stay as close to his owner as possible, especially in strange surroundings. When your puppy sees you moving away, his natural inclination will be to get close to you. This is a perfect time to use the come command.

If you are a patient and flexible teacher, your Collie pup will be able to learn any command.

Later, as a puppy grows more self-confident and independent, you may want to attach a long leash or rope to the puppy's collar to ensure the correct response. Again, do not chase or punish your puppy for not obeying the come command. Doing so in the initial stages of training makes the youngster associate the command with something to fear and this will result in avoidance rather than the immediate positive response you desire. It is imperative that you praise your puppy and give him a treat when he does come to you, even if he voluntarily delays responding for many minutes.

The Sit and Stay Commands

Just as important to your Collie's safety (and your sanity!) as the no command and learning to come when called are the sit and stay commands. Even very young puppies can learn the sit command quickly, especially if it appears to be a game and a food treat is involved.

Your puppy should always be on a collar and leash for his lessons. A young puppy is not beyond getting up and walking away when he has decided you and your lessons are boring.

Give the sit command immediately before pushing down on your puppy's hindquarters or before you scoop his hind legs under him to mold him into a sit position. Praise the puppy lavishly when he does sit, even though it is you who made the action take place. Again, a food treat always seems to get the lesson across to the learning youngster.

Continue holding the dog's rear end down and repeat the sit command several times. If your dog makes an attempt to get up, repeat the command yet again while exerting pressure on the rear end until the correct position is assumed. Make your Collie stay in this position for increasing lengths of time. Begin with a few seconds and increase the time as lessons progress over the following weeks.

This handsome pair of Rough Collies has earned almost every obedience title offered, proving beauty and brains go hand in hand (or in this case, paw in paw).

Should your young student attempt to get up or to lie down, he should be corrected by simply saying "Sit!" in a firm voice. This should be accompanied by returning the dog to the desired position. Only when you decide your dog should get up should he be allowed to do so. Do not test a very young puppy's patience to the limits. Remember you are dealing with a baby. The attention span of any youngster, canine or human, is relatively short.

When you do decide your puppy can get up, call his name, say "OK" and make a big fuss over him. Praise and a food treat are in order every time your puppy responds correctly.

Once your puppy has mastered the sit lesson, you may start on the stay command. With your dog on leash and facing you, command him to sit, then take a step or two back. If your dog attempts to get up to follow, firmly say, "Sit, stay!" While you are saying this raise your hand, palm toward the dog, and again command "Stay!"

Any attempt on your dog's part to get up must be corrected at once, returning him to the sit position and repeating, "Stay!"

Every puppy can benefit from basic obedience training. This Collie pup masters the "sit" command.

Once your Collie begins to understand what you want, you can gradually increase the distance you step back. With a long leash attached to your dog's collar (even a clothesline will do) start with a few steps and gradually increase the distance to several yards. Your Collie must eventually learn the sit, stay command must be obeyed no matter how far away you are. Later on, with advanced training, your dog will learn the command is to be obeyed even when you move entirely out of sight.

As your Collie masters this lesson and is able to remain in the sit position for as long as you dictate, avoid calling the dog to you at first. This makes the dog overly anxious to get up and run to you. Instead, walk back to your dog and say "OK," a signal that the command is over. Later, when your Collie becomes more reliable in this respect, you can call him to you.

The sit, stay lesson can take considerable time and patience, especially with a puppy whose attention span will be very short. It is best to keep the stay part of the lesson to a minimum until the puppy is at least five or six months old. Everything in a very young Collie's makeup urges him to stay close to you wherever you go. Forcing a very young puppy to operate against his natural instincts can be bewildering.

The Down Command

Once your Collie has mastered the sit and stay commands, you may begin work on down. This is the single word command for lie down. Use the down command only when you want the dog to lie *Hand signals in conjunction with verbal commands are very effective when training your Collie. Cullen owned by Sally Richardson practices his down/stay.*

Collies love to please their master and take to obedience work easily. Katie and owner Kathy Warner do a demonstration for their local kennel club's anniversary.

down. If you want your dog to get off your sofa or to stop jumping up on people, use the off command. Do not interchange these two commands. Doing so will only serve to confuse your dog and evoking the right response will become next to impossible.

The down position is especially useful if you want your Collie to remain in a particular place for a long period of time. A dog is usually far more inclined to stay put when he is lying down than when he is sitting. Teaching this command to your Collie may take more time and patience than the previous lessons. It is believed by some animal behaviorists that assuming the down position somehow represents submissiveness to the dog.

With your dog sitting in front and facing you, hold a treat in your right hand with the excess part of the leash in your left hand. Hold the treat under the dog's nose and slowly bring your hand down to the ground. Your dog will follow the treat with his head and neck. As he does, give the command "down" and exert light pressure on the dog's shoulders with your left

hand. If your dog resists the pressure on his shoulders, do not continue pushing down, as doing so will only create more resistance.

An alternative method of getting your Collie headed into the down position is to move around to the dog's right side and as you draw his attention downward with your right hand, slide your left hand or arm under the dog's front legs and gently slide them forward. In the case of a very young Collie puppy, you will undoubtedly have to be on your knees next to the youngster.

With practice, persistence, and praise, your Collie is capable of learning the most difficult of tricks.

As your dog's forelegs begin to slide out to his front, keep moving the treat along the ground until the dog's whole body is lying on the ground while you continually repeat "down." Once your Collie has assumed the position you desire, give him the treat and a lot of praise. Continue assisting your dog into the down position until he does so on his own. Be firm, be patient, and be prepared for those occasional "I have no idea what you mean" looks your Collie student may give you.

The Heel Command

In learning to heel, your dog will walk on your left side with his shoulder next to your leg, no matter which direction you might go or how quickly you turn. Teaching your Collie to heel will not only make your daily walks far more enjoyable, it will make a far more tractable companion when the two of you are in crowded or confusing situations.

We have found a lightweight link-chain training collar is very useful for the heeling lesson. It provides both quick pressure around the neck and a snapping sound, both of which get the dog's attention. Erroneously referred to as a "choke collar," the link-chain collar used properly does not choke the dog. The pet shop where you purchase the training collar

Teaching your Collie to heel will make your daily walks a more enjoyable experience.

will be able to show you the proper way to put this collar on your dog. Do not leave this collar on your puppy when training sessions are finished. Puppies are ingenious at getting their lower jaw or legs caught in the training chain. Changing to the link-chain collar at training time also signals your Collie that it is time to get down to the business at hand.

When you begin training your puppy to walk along on the leash, you should accustom the youngster to walk on your left side. The leash should cross your body from the dog's collar to your right hand. The excess portion of the leash will be folded into your right hand and your left hand will be used to make corrections with the leash. A quick short jerk on the leash with your left hand will keep your dog from lunging side to side, pulling ahead or lagging back. As you make a correction, give the "heel" command. Keep the leash slack as long as your dog maintains the proper position at your side.

If your Collie begins to drift away, give the leash a sharp jerk, guide the dog back to the correct position, and give the "heel" command. Do not pull on the lead with steady pressure. What is needed is a sharp but gentle jerking motion to get your dog's attention.

TRAINING CLASSES

There are few limits to what a patient consistent Collie owner can teach his or her dog. For advanced obedience work beyond the basics, however, it is wise for the inexperienced owner to consider local professional assistance. Professional trainers have had long-standing experience in avoiding the pitfalls of obedience training and can help you to avoid these mistakes as well. This training assistance can be obtained in many ways. Classes are particularly good for your Collie's socialization and attentiveness. The dog will learn that he must obey even when there are other dogs and people around that

Whether a cart puller, backpacker, or best friend, there is no limit to the talents of the Collie.

provide the temptation to run off and play. There are free-of-charge classes at many parks and recreation facilities, as well as very formal and sometimes very expensive individual lessons with private trainers. There are also some obedience schools that will take your Collie and train him for you. However, unless your schedule provides no time at all to train your own dog, having someone else train your Collie for you would be last on our list of recommendations. The rapport that develops between the owner who has trained his or her own Collie to be a pleasant companion and good canine citizen is very special—

Puppies have a short attention span, so keep training sessions short and be sure to praise him lavishly when finished.

well worth the time and patience it requires to achieve.

Training classes are not only a great place for your Collie to learn basic obedience; it also gives him a chance to socialize with other dogs.

VERSATILITY

The Collie's intelligence, energy, stamina, and desire to please has led to a variety of

highly specialized roles. Many Collies have become hearing and sight dogs. The Collie trained in this manner can be used in the home to help the hearing impaired by alerting the person that the door bell or telephone has rung. Sight assistance dogs can be trained to locate objects or help their restricted-vision owners to avoid falls. Collies also make excellent therapy dogs. They love people and are extremely successful in providing retirement home residents and hospital patients with the feeling that someone really cares about them. Collies, of course, love children and when the dogs make appearances at children's hospitals, the youngsters are absolutely delighted.

Collies can make top obedience dogs. Their strong desire to please and willingness to work make them a fun dog to train. They are ringside favorites in that the dogs are such happy workers. The ringside is always happy to cheer the "Lassie dog" on to victory.

Once your Collie learns basic obedience, he can go on to compete in more difficult events such as agility. Raisin owned by Charlotte Coviak clears the bar jump.

Love, praise, and affection are the best training motivators for your Collie.

Collies are very agile and seem to particularly enjoy working their way through all the agility course obstacles. Again, they are extremely popular with the ringside.

As a herding dog, Collies have been trained to both formal trialing standards and to actually work livestock on farms throughout the country. The beauty of this breed performing in the capacity for which he was created has few equals.

There is actually no boundary to this beautiful breed's versatility. If the Collie has any limitations at all they are usually due to human limitations. Above all, however, Collies are ideal companions and friends. Through the ages the Collie has been a worker, a guard, and a companion to mankind. Through the efforts of dedicated breeders and guardians of the breed, the Collie has remained consistently popular. This is a breed eager and willing to please, one that never needs a rough hand to develop his intelligence and versatility. Those are qualities that are part of his heritage and are given freely to the families they love.

SPORT of
Purebred Dogs *by Judy Iby*

Welcome to the exciting and sometimes frustrating sport of dogs. No doubt you are trying to learn more about dogs or you wouldn't be deep into this book. This section covers the basics that may entice you, further your knowledge and help you to understand the dog world.

Dog showing has been a very popular sport for a long time and has been taken quite seriously by some. Others only enjoy it as a hobby.

The Kennel Club in England was formed in 1859, the American Kennel Club was established in 1884 and the Canadian Kennel Club was formed in 1888. The purpose of these clubs was to register purebred dogs and maintain their Stud Books. In the beginning, the concept of registering dogs was not readily accepted. More than 36 million dogs have been enrolled in the AKC Stud Book since its inception in 1888. Presently the kennel clubs not only register dogs but adopt and enforce rules and regulations governing dog shows, obedience trials and field trials. Over the years they have fostered and encouraged interest in the health and welfare of the purebred dog. They routinely donate funds to veterinary research for study on genetic disorders.

Successful showing takes dedication and preparation, but most of all, it should be an enjoyable experience for both owners and dogs alike.

Below are the addresses of the kennel clubs in the United States, Great Britain and Canada.

The American Kennel Club
51 Madison Avenue
New York, NY 10010
(Their registry is located at: 5580 Centerview Drive, STE 200, Raleigh, NC 27606-3390)

The Kennel Club
1 Clarges Street
Piccadilly, London, WIY 8AB, England

The Canadian Kennel Club
111 Eglinton Avenue
East Toronto, Ontario M6S 4V7
Canada

Training to compete is not an easy task, but the satisfaction you'll receive when you accomplish your goals is rewarding for both you and your Collie.

Today there are numerous activities that are enjoyable for both the dog and the handler. Some of the activities include conformation showing, obedience competition, tracking, agility, the Canine Good Citizen Certificate, and a wide range of instinct tests that vary from breed to breed. Where you start depends upon your goals which early on may not be readily apparent.

PUPPY KINDERGARTEN

Every puppy will benefit from this class. PKT is the foundation for all future dog activities from conformation to "couch potatoes." Pet owners should make an effort to attend even if they never expect to show their dog. The class is designed for puppies about three months of age with graduation at approximately five months of age. All the puppies will be in the same age group and, even though some may be a little unruly, there should not be any real problem. This class will teach the puppy some beginning obedience. As in all obedience classes the owner learns how to train his own dog. The PKT class gives the puppy the opportunity to interact with other puppies in the same age group and exposes him to strangers, which is very important. Some dogs grow up with behavior problems, one of them being fear of strangers. As you can see, there can be much to gain from this class.

There are some basic obedience exercises that every dog should learn. Some of these can be started with puppy kindergarten.

CONFORMATION

Conformation showing is our oldest dog show sport. This type of showing is based on the dog's appearance—that is his structure, movement and attitude. When considering this type of showing, you need to be aware of your breed's standard and be able to evaluate your dog compared to that standard. The breeder of your puppy or other experienced breeders would be good sources for such an evaluation. Puppies can go through lots of changes over a period of time. Many puppies start out as promising hopefuls and then after maturing may be disappointing as show candidates. Even so this should not deter them from being excellent pets.

Usually conformation training classes are offered by the local kennel or obedience clubs. These are excellent places for training puppies. The puppy should be able to walk on a lead before entering such a class. Proper ring procedure and technique for posing (stacking) the dog will be demonstrated as well as gaiting the dog. Usually certain patterns are used in the ring such as the triangle or the "L." Conformation class, like the PKT class, will give your youngster the opportunity to socialize with different breeds of dogs and humans too.

It takes some time to learn the routine of conformation showing. Usually one starts at the puppy matches that may be AKC Sanctioned or Fun Matches. These matches are generally for puppies from two or three months to a year old, and there may be classes for the adult over the age of 12 months. Similar to point shows, the classes are divided by sex and after completion of the classes in that breed or variety, the class winners compete for Best of Breed or Variety. The winner goes on to compete in the Group and the Group winners compete for Best in Match. No championship points are awarded for match wins.

A few matches can be great training for puppies even though there is no intention to go on showing. Matches enable the puppy to meet new people and be handled by a stranger—the judge. It is also a change of environment, which broadens the horizon for both dog and handler. Matches and other dog activities boost the confidence of the handler and especially the younger handlers.

Earning an AKC championship is built on a point system, which is different from Great Britain. To become an AKC Champion of Record the dog must earn 15 points. The number of points earned each time depends upon the number of dogs in competition. The number of points available at each show depends upon the breed, its sex and the location of the show. The United States is divided into ten AKC zones. Each zone has its own set of points.

In conformation, your Collie will be evaluated on how closely he conforms to the breed standard.

The purpose of the zones is to try to equalize the points available from breed to breed and area to area. The AKC adjusts the point scale annually.

The number of points that can be won at a show are between one and five. Three-, four- and five-point wins are considered majors. Not only does the dog need 15 points won under three different judges, but those points must include two majors under two different judges. Canada also works on a point system but majors are not required.

Dogs always show before bitches. The classes available to those seeking points are: Puppy (which may be divided into 6 to 9 months and 9 to 12 months); 12 to 18 months; Novice; Bred-by-Exhibitor; American-bred; and Open. The class winners of the same sex of each breed or variety compete against each other for Winners Dog and Winners Bitch. A

Reserve Winners Dog and Reserve Winners Bitch are also awarded but do not carry any points unless the Winners win is disallowed by AKC. The Winners Dog and Bitch compete with the specials (those dogs that have attained championship) for Best of Breed or Variety, Best of Winners and Best of Opposite Sex. It is possible to pick up an extra point or even a major if the points are higher for the defeated winner than those of Best of Winners. The latter would get the higher total from the defeated winner.

At an all-breed show, each Best of Breed or Variety winner will go on to his respective Group and then the Group winners will compete against each other for Best in Show. There are seven Groups: Sporting, Hounds, Working, Terriers, Toys, Non-Sporting and Herding. Obviously there are no Groups at speciality shows (those shows that have only one breed or a show such as the American Spaniel Club's Flushing Spaniel Show, which is for all flushing spaniel breeds).

Obedience training allows the Collie and his owner to develop a closeness formed from working together.

Earning a championship in England is somewhat different since they do not have a point system. Challenge Certificates are awarded if the judge feels the dog is deserving regardless of the number of dogs in competition. A dog must earn three Challenge Certificates under three different judges, with at least one of these Certificates being won after the age of 12 months. Competition is very strong and entries may be higher than they are in the U.S. The Kennel Club's Challenge Certificates are only available at Championship Shows.

In England, The Kennel Club regulations require that certain dogs, Border Collies and Gundog breeds, qualify in a working capacity (i.e., obedience or field

Ch. Waltstone Gay Caprice owned by Ruth and Walter Ecker.

trials) before becoming a full Champion. If they do not qualify in the working aspect, then they are designated a Show Champion, which is equivalent to the AKC's Champion of Record. A Gundog may be granted the title of Field Trial Champion (FT Ch.) if it passes all the tests in the field but would also have to qualify in conformation before becoming a full Champion. A Border Collie that earns the title of Obedience Champion (Ob Ch.) must also qualify in the conformation ring before becoming a Champion.

The U.S. doesn't have a designation full Champion but does award for Dual and Triple Champions. The Dual Champion must be a Champion of Record, and either Champion Tracker, Herding Champion, Obedience Trial Champion or Field Champion. Any dog that has been awarded the titles of Champion of Record, and any two of the following: Champion Tracker, Herding Champion, Obedience Trial Champion or Field Champion, may be designated as a Triple Champion.

The shows in England seem to put more emphasis on breeder judges than those in the U.S. There is much competition within the breeds. Therefore the quality of the individual breeds should be very good. In the United States we tend to have more "all around judges" (those that judge multiple breeds) and use the breeder judges at the specialty shows. Breeder judges are more familiar with their own breed since they are actively breeding that breed or did so at one time. Americans emphasize Group and Best in Show wins and promote them accordingly.

The shows in England can be very large and extend over several days, with the Groups being scheduled on different days. Though multi-day shows are not common in the U.S., there are cluster shows, where several different clubs will use the same show site over consecutive days.

Westminster Kennel Club is our most prestigious show although the entry is limited to 2500. In recent years, entry has been limited to Champions. This show is more formal than the majority of the shows with the judges wearing formal attire and the handlers fashionably dressed. In most instances the quality of the dogs is superb. After all, it is a show of Champions. It is a good show to study the AKC registered breeds and is by far the most exciting—especially since it is televised! WKC is one of the few shows in this country that is still benched. This means the dog must be in his benched area during the show hours except when he is being groomed, in the ring, or being exercised.

Typically, the handlers are very particular about their appearances. They are careful not to wear something that will detract from their dog but will perhaps enhance it. American ring procedure is quite formal compared to that of other countries. There is a certain etiquette expected between the judge and exhibitor and among the other exhibitors. Of course it is not always the case but the judge is supposed to be polite, not engaging in small talk or acknowledging how well he knows the handler. There is a more informal and relaxed atmosphere at the shows in other countries. For instance, the dress code is more casual. I can see where this might be more fun for the exhibitor and especially for the novice. The U.S. is very handler-oriented in many of the breeds. It is true, in most instances, that the experienced professional handler can present the dog better and will have a feel for what a judge likes.

Handlers should wear comfortable clothing that complements the dog and allows them to move freely in the ring.

In England, Crufts is The Kennel Club's own show and is most assuredly the largest dog show in the world. They've been known to have an entry of nearly 20,000, and the show lasts four days. Entry is only gained by qualifying through winning in specified classes at another Championship Show. Westminster is strictly conformation, but Crufts exhibitors and spectators enjoy not only conformation but obedience, agility and a multitude of exhibitions as well. Obedience was admitted in 1957 and agility in 1983.

If you are handling your own dog, please give some consideration to your apparel. For sure the dress code at matches is more informal than the point shows. However, you should wear something a little more appropriate than beach attire or ragged jeans and bare feet. If you check out the handlers and see what is presently fashionable, you'll catch on. Men usually dress with a shirt and tie and a nice sports coat. Whether you are male or female, you will want to wear comfortable clothes and shoes. You need to be able to run with your dog and you certainly don't want to take a chance of falling and hurting yourself. Heaven forbid, if nothing else, you'll upset your dog. Women usually wear a dress or two-piece outfit, preferably with pockets to carry bait, comb, brush, etc. In this case men are the lucky ones with all their pockets. Ladies, think about where your dress will be if you need to kneel on the floor and also think about running. Does it allow freedom to do so?

With training, who knows how far your Collie puppy can go? Five-month-old Maighdlin Country Calico owned by Lois and Rob Baylor.

You need to take along dog; crate; ex pen (if you use one); extra newspaper; water pail and water; all required grooming equipment, including hair dryer and extension cord; table; chair for you; bait for dog and lunch for you and friends; and, last but not least, clean up materials, such as plastic bags, paper towels, and perhaps a bath towel and some shampoo—just in case. Don't forget your entry confirmation and directions to the show.

If you are showing in obedience, then you will want to wear pants. Many of our top obedience handlers wear pants that are color-coordinated with their dogs. The philosophy is that imperfections in the black dog will be less obvious next to your black pants.

Whether you are showing in conformation, Junior Showmanship or obedience, you need to watch the clock and be sure you are not late. It is customary to pick up your conformation armband a few minutes before the start of the

A Canine Good Citizen will be able to get along with people—especially children. Ch. Maighdlin Conor MacLain at four months of age with friend Soren Beiler.

class. They will not wait for you and if you are on the show grounds and not in the ring, you will upset everyone. It's a little more complicated picking up your obedience armband if you show later in the class. If you have not picked up your armband and they get to your number, you may not be allowed to show. It's best to pick up your armband early, but then you may show earlier than expected if other handlers don't pick up. Customarily all conflicts should be discussed with the judge prior to the start of the class.

An exercise pen is just one of the pieces of equipment you will need to bring with you to a dog show.

Junior Showmanship

The Junior Showmanship Class is a wonderful way to build self confidence even if there are no aspirations of staying with the dog-show game later in life. Frequently, Junior Showmanship becomes the background of those who become successful exhibitors/handlers in the future. In some instances it is taken very seriously, and success is measured in terms of wins. The Junior Handler is judged solely on his ability and skill in presenting his dog. The dog's conformation is not to be considered by the judge. Even so the condition and grooming of the dog may be a reflection upon the handler.

Usually the matches and point shows include different classes. The Junior Handler's dog may be entered in a breed or obedience class and even shown by another person in that class. Junior Showmanship classes are usually divided by age and perhaps sex. The age is determined by the handler's age on the day of the show.

Canine Good Citizen

The AKC sponsors a program to encourage dog owners to train their dogs. Local clubs perform the pass/fail tests, and dogs who pass are awarded a Canine Good Citizen Certificate. Proof of vaccination is required at the time of participation. The test includes:

1. Accepting a friendly stranger.
2. Sitting politely for petting.
3. Appearance and grooming.
4. Walking on a loose leash.
5. Walking through a crowd.
6. Sit and down on command/staying in place.
7. Come when called.
8. Reaction to another dog.
9. Reactions to distractions.
10. Supervised separation.

If more effort was made by pet owners to accomplish these exercises, fewer dogs would be cast off to the humane shelter.

Ch. Windarla's World Seeker owned by Marlene and Ewing Nicholson.

Obedience

Obedience is necessary, without a doubt, but it can also become a wonderful hobby or even an obsession. Obedience classes and competition can provide wonderful companionship, not only with your dog but with your classmates or fellow competitors. It is always gratifying to discuss your dog's problems with others who have had similar experiences. The AKC acknowledged Obedience around 1936, and it has changed tremendously even though many of the exercises are basically the same. Today, obedience competition is just that—very competitive. Even so, it is possible for every obedience exhibitor to come home a winner (by earning qualifying scores) even though he/she may not earn a placement in the class.

Most of the obedience titles are awarded after earning three qualifying scores (legs) in the appropriate class under three different judges. These classes offer a perfect score of 200, which is extremely rare. Each of the class exercises has its own point value. A leg is earned after receiving a score of at least 170 and at least 50 percent of the points available in each exercise. The titles are:

Companion Dog—CD
This is called the Novice Class and the exercises are:

1.	Heel on leash and figure 8	40 points
2.	Stand for examination	30 points
3.	Heel free	40 points
4.	Recall	30 points
5.	Long sit—one minute	30 points
6.	Long down—three minutes	30 points
	Maximum total score	200 points

Companion Dog Excellent—CDX
This is the Open Class and the exercises are:

1.	Heel off leash and figure 8	40 points
2.	Drop on recall	30 points
3.	Retrieve on flat	20 points
4.	Retrieve over high jump	30 points
5.	Broad jump	20 points
6.	Long sit—three minutes (out of sight)	30 points
7.	Long down—five minutes (out of sight)	30 points
	Maximum total score	200 points

Utility Dog—UD
The Utility Class exercises are:

1.	Signal Exercise	40 points
2.	Scent discrimination-Article 1	30 points
3.	Scent discrimination-Article 2	30 points
4.	Directed retrieve	30 points
5.	Moving stand and examination	30 points
6.	Directed jumping	40 points
	Maximum total score	200 points

After achieving the UD title, you may feel inclined to go after the UDX and/or OTCh. The UDX (Utility Dog Excellent) title went into effect in January 1994. It is not easily attained. The title requires qualifying simultaneously ten times in Open B and Utility B but not necessarily at consecutive shows.

The OTCh (Obedience Trial Champion) is awarded after the dog has earned his UD and then goes on to earn 100 championship points, a first place in Utility, a first place in Open and another first place in either class. The placements must be won under three different judges at all-breed obedience trials. The points are determined by the number of dogs competing in the Open B and Utility B classes. The OTCh title precedes the dog's name.

Obedience matches (AKC Sanctioned, Fun, and Show and Go) are usually available. Usually they are sponsored by the local obedience clubs. When preparing an obedience dog for a title, you will find matches very helpful. Fun Matches and Show and Go Matches are more lenient in allowing you to make corrections in the ring. This type of training is usually very necessary for the Open and Utility Classes. AKC Sanctioned Obedience Matches do not allow

Scent discrimination is one of the many events in which the versatile Collie can compete.

corrections in the ring since they must abide by the AKC Obedience Regulations. If you are interested in showing in obedience, then you should contact the AKC for a copy of the Obedience Regulations.

TRACKING

Tracking is officially classified obedience. There are three tracking titles available: Tracking Dog (TD), Tracking Dog Excellent (TDX), Variable Surface Tracking (VST). If all three tracking titles are obtained, then the dog officially becomes a CT (Champion Tracker). The CT will go in front of the dog's name.

A TD may be earned anytime and does not have to follow the other obedience titles. There are many exhibitors that prefer tracking to obedience, and there are others who do both.

The athletic and nimble Collie excels in agility competitions.

Agility is an action-packed sport that is thrill for both the dogs and spectators alike.

AGILITY

Agility was first introduced by John Varley in England at the Crufts Dog Show, February 1978, but Peter Meanwell, competitor and judge, actually developed the idea. It was officially recognized in the early '80s. Agility is extremely popular in England and Canada and growing in popularity in the U.S. The AKC acknowledged agility in August 1994. Dogs must be at least 12 months of age to be entered. It is a fascinating sport that the dog, handler and spectators enjoy to the utmost. Agility is a spectator sport! The dog performs off lead. The handler either runs with his dog or positions himself on the course and directs his dog with verbal and hand signals over a timed course over or through a variety of obstacles including a time out or pause. One of the main drawbacks to agility is finding a place to train. The obstacles take up a lot of space and it is very time consuming to put up and take down courses.

The titles earned at AKC agility trials are Novice Agility Dog (NAD), Open Agility Dog (OAD), Agility Dog Excellent (ADX), and Master Agility Excellent (MAX). In order to acquire an agility title, a dog must earn a qualifying score in its respective class on three separate occasions under two different judges. The MAX will be awarded after earning ten qualifying scores in the Agility Excellent Class.

PERFORMANCE TESTS

During the last decade the American Kennel Club has promoted performance tests–those events that test the different breeds' natural abilities. This type of event encourages a handler to devote even more time to his dog and retain the natural instincts of his breed heritage. It is an important part of the wonderful world of dogs.

Herding Titles

For all Herding breeds and Rottweilers and Samoyeds.

Entrants must be at least nine months of age and dogs with limited registration (ILP) are eligible. The Herding program is divided into Testing and Trial sections. The goal is to demonstrate proficiency in herding livestock in diverse situations. The titles offered are Herding Started (HS), Herding Intermediate (HI), and Herding Excellent (HX). Upon completion of the HX a Herding Championship may be earned after accumulating 15 championship points.

The above information has been taken from the AKC Guidelines for the appropriate events.

GENERAL INFORMATION

Obedience, tracking and agility allow the purebred dog with an Indefinite Listing Privilege (ILP) number or a limited registration to be exhibited and earn titles. Application must be made to the AKC for an ILP number.

The American Kennel Club publishes a monthly *Events* magazine that is part of the *Gazette*, their official journal for the sport of purebred dogs. The *Events* section lists upcoming shows and the secretary or superintendent for them. The majority of the conformation shows in the U.S. are overseen by licensed superintendents. Generally the entry closing date is approximately two-and-a-half weeks before the actual show. Point shows are fairly expensive, while the match shows cost about one third of the point show entry fee. Match shows usually take entries the day of the show but some are pre-entry. The best way to find match show information is through your local kennel club. Upon asking, the AKC can provide you with a list of superintendents, and you can write and ask to be put on their mailing lists.

Obedience trial and tracking test information is available through the AKC. Frequently these events are not superintended, but put on by the host club. Therefore you would make the entry with the event's secretary.

As you have read, there are numerous activities you can share with your dog. Regardless what you do, it does take teamwork. Your dog can only benefit from your attention and training. We hope this chapter has enlightened you and hope, if nothing else, you will attend a show here and there. Perhaps you will start with a puppy kindergarten class, and who knows where it may lead!

Herding trials allow the Collie to use his inherent talents and retain his natural instincts. Ch. Tee Creek's Already Gone is determined to get his ducks in a row.

HEALTH CARE *by Judy Iby*

Veterinary medicine has become far more sophisticated than what was available to our ancestors. This can be attributed to the increase in household pets and consequently the demand for better care for them. Also human medicine has become far more complex. Today diagnostic testing in veterinary medicine parallels human diagnostics. Because of better technology we can expect our pets to live healthier lives thereby increasing their life spans.

THE FIRST CHECK UP

Your Collie will need regular checkups to maintain his good health and prevent potential problems.

You will want to take your new puppy/dog in for its first check up within 48 to 72 hours after acquiring it. Many breeders strongly recommend this check up and so do the humane shelters. A puppy/dog can appear healthy but it may have a serious problem that is not apparent to the layman. Most pets have some type of a minor flaw that may never cause a real problem.

Unfortunately if he/she should have a serious problem, you will want to consider the consequences of keeping the pet and the attachments that will be formed, which may be broken prematurely. Keep in mind there are many healthy dogs looking for good homes.

This first check up is a good time to establish yourself with the veterinarian and learn the office policy regarding their hours and how they handle emergencies. Usually the breeder or another conscientious pet owner is a good reference for locating a capable veterinarian. You should be aware that not all veterinarians give the same quality of service. Please do not make your selection on the least expensive clinic, as they may be short changing your pet. There is the possibility that eventually it will cost you more due to improper diagnosis, treatment, etc. If you are selecting a new veterinarian, feel free to ask for a tour of the clinic. You should inquire about making an appointment for a tour since all clinics are working clinics, and therefore may not be available all day for sightseers. You

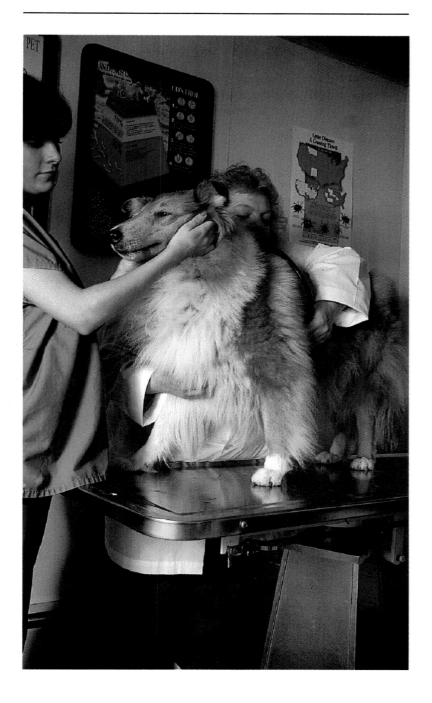

may worry less if you see where your pet will be spending the day if he ever needs to be hospitalized.

THE PHYSICAL EXAM

Your veterinarian will check your pet's overall condition, which includes listening to the heart; checking the respiration; feeling the abdomen, muscles and joints; checking the mouth, which includes the gum color and signs of gum disease along with plaque buildup; checking the ears for signs of an infection or ear mites; examining the eyes; and, last but not least, checking the condition of the skin and coat.

He should ask you questions regarding your pet's eating and elimination habits and invite you to relay your questions. It is a good idea to prepare a list so as not to forget anything. He should discuss the proper diet and the quantity to be fed. If this should differ from your breeder's recommendation, then you should convey to him the breeder's choice and see if he approves. If he recommends changing the diet, then this should be done over a few days so as not to cause a gastrointestinal upset. It is customary to take in a fresh stool sample (just a small amount) for a test for intestinal parasites. It must be fresh, preferably within 12 hours, since the eggs hatch quickly and after hatching will not be observed under the microscope. If your pet isn't obliging then, usually the technician can take one in the clinic.

IMMUNIZATIONS

It is important that you take your puppy/dog's vaccination record with you on your first visit. In case of a puppy, presumably the breeder has seen to the vaccinations up to the time you acquired custody. Veterinarians differ in their

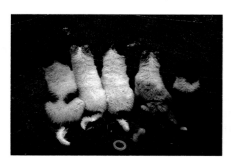

vaccination protocol. It is not unusual for your puppy to have received vaccinations for

Collie puppies cannot become strong healthy adults without consistent health care and maintenance.

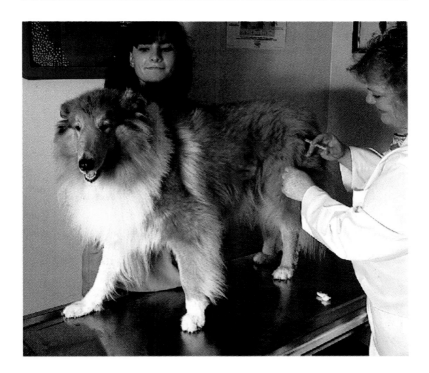

Your veterinarian will put your Collie puppy on a vaccination schedule when he is a puppy and then he will need regular booster shots to prevent disease.
distemper, hepatitis, leptospirosis, parvovirus and parainfluenza every two to three weeks from the age of five or six weeks. Usually this is a combined injection and is typically called the DHLPP. The DHLPP is given through at least 12 to 14 weeks of age, and it is customary to continue with another parvovirus vaccine at 16 to 18 weeks. You may wonder why so many immunizations are necessary. No one knows for sure when the puppy's maternal antibodies are gone, although it is customarily accepted that distemper antibodies are gone by 12 weeks. Usually parvovirus antibodies are gone by 16 to 18 weeks of age. However, it is possible for the maternal antibodies to be gone at a much earlier age or even a later age. Therefore immunizations are started at an early age. The vaccine will not give immunity as long as there are maternal antibodies.

The rabies vaccination is given at three or six months of age depending on your local laws. A vaccine for bordetella (kennel cough) is advisable and can be given anytime from the age of five weeks. The coronavirus is not commonly given unless there is a problem locally. The Lyme vaccine is necessary in endemic areas. Lyme disease has been reported in 47 states.

Distemper

This is virtually an incurable disease. If the dog recovers, he is subject to severe nervous disorders. The virus attacks every tissue in the body and resembles a bad cold with a fever. It can cause a runny nose and eyes and cause gastrointestinal disorders, including a poor appetite, vomiting and diarrhea. The virus is carried by raccoons, foxes, wolves, mink and other dogs. Unvaccinated youngsters and senior citizens are very susceptible. This is still a common disease.

Collies can pick up parasites outside or from other dogs. Make sure your puppy has his proper immunizations before taking him out to make friends.

Hepatitis

This is a virus that is most serious in very young dogs. It is spread by contact with an infected animal or its stool or urine. The virus affects the liver and kidneys and is characterized by high fever, depression and lack of appetite. Recovered animals may be afflicted with chronic illnesses.

A young puppy is very vulnerable and will need to see a veterinarian within 48 hours of his arrival in your new home.

Leptospirosis

This is a bacterial disease transmitted by contact with the urine of an infected dog, rat or other wildlife. It produces severe symptoms of fever, depression, jaundice and internal bleeding and was fatal before the vaccine was developed. Recovered dogs can be carriers, and the disease can be transmitted from dogs to humans.

Parvovirus

This was first noted in the late 1970s and is still a fatal disease. However, with proper vaccinations, early diagnosis and prompt treatment, it is a manageable disease. It attacks the bone marrow and intestinal tract. The symptoms include depression, loss of appetite, vomiting, diarrhea and collapse. Immediate medical attention is of the essence.

Rabies

This is shed in the saliva and is carried by raccoons, skunks, foxes, other dogs and cats. It attacks nerve tissue, resulting in paralysis and death. Rabies can be transmitted to people and is virtually always fatal. This disease is reappearing in the suburbs.

Bordetella (Kennel Cough)

The symptoms are coughing, sneezing, hacking and retching accompanied by nasal discharge usually lasting from a few days to several weeks. There are several disease-producing organisms responsible for this disease. The present vaccines are helpful but do not protect for all the strains. It usually is not life threatening but in some instances it can progress to a serious bronchopneumonia. The disease is highly contagious. The vaccination should be given routinely for dogs that come in contact with other dogs, such as through boarding, training class or visits to the groomer.

Coronavirus

This is usually self limiting and not life threatening. It was first noted in the late '70s about a year before parvovirus. The virus produces a yellow/brown stool and there may be depression, vomiting and diarrhea.

Lyme Disease

This was first diagnosed in the United States in 1976 in Lyme, CT in people who lived in close proximity to the deer tick. Symptoms may include acute lameness, fever, swelling of joints and loss of appetite. Your veterinarian can advise you if you live in an endemic area.

After your puppy has completed his puppy vaccinations, you will continue to booster the DHLPP once a year. It is customary to booster the rabies one year after the first vaccine and then, depending on where you live, it should be boostered every year or every three years. This depends on your local laws. The Lyme and corona vaccines are boostered annually and it is recommended that the bordetella be boostered every six to eight months.

Annual Visit

I would like to impress the importance of the annual check up, which would include the booster vaccinations, check for intestinal parasites and test for heartworm. Today in our very busy world it is rush, rush and see "how much you can get for how little." Unbelievably, some non-veterinary businesses have entered into the vaccination business. More harm than good can come to your dog through improper vaccinations, possibly from inferior vaccines and/or the wrong schedule. More than likely you truly care about your companion dog and over the years you have devoted much time and expense to his well being. Perhaps you are unaware that a vaccination is not just a vaccination. There is more involved. Please, please follow through with regular physical examinations. It is so important for your veterinarian to know your dog and this is especially true during middle age through the geriatric years. More than likely your older dog will require more than one physical a year. The annual physical is good preventive medicine. Through early diagnosis and subsequent treatment your dog can maintain a longer and better quality of life.

Intestinal Parasites

Hookworms

These are almost microscopic intestinal worms that can cause anemia and therefore serious problems, including death, in young puppies. Hookworms can be transmitted to humans through penetration of the skin. Puppies may be born with them.

Roundworm eggs as seen on a fecal evaluation. The eggs must develop for a least 12 days before they are infective.

Roundworms

These are spaghetti-like worms that can cause a potbellied appearance and dull coat along with more severe symptoms, such as vomiting, diarrhea and coughing. Puppies acquire these while in the mother's uterus and through lactation. Both hookworms and roundworms may be acquired through ingestion.

Whipworms

These have a three-month life cycle and are not acquired through the dam. They cause intermittent diarrhea usually with mucus. Whipworms are possibly the most difficult worm to eradicate. Their eggs are very resistant to most environmental factors and can last for years until the proper conditions enable them to mature. Whipworms are seldom seen in the stool.

Intestinal parasites are more prevalent in some areas than others. Climate, soil and contamination are big factors contributing to the incidence of intestinal parasites. Eggs are passed in the stool, lay on the ground and then become infective in a certain number of days. Each of the above worms has a different life cycle. Your best chance of becoming and remaining worm-free is to always pooper-scoop your yard. A fenced-in yard keeps stray dogs out, which is certainly helpful.

I would recommend having a fecal examination on your dog twice a year or more often if there is a problem. If your dog has a positive fecal sample, then he will be given the appropriate medication and you will be asked to bring back another stool sample in a certain period of time (depending on the type of worm) and then be rewormed. This process goes on until he has at least two negative samples. The different types of worms require different medications. You will be wasting your money and doing your dog an injustice by buying over-the-counter medication without first consulting your veterinarian.

OTHER INTERNAL PARASITES

Coccidiosis and Giardiasis

These protozoal infections usually affect puppies, especially in places where large numbers of puppies are brought together. Older dogs may harbor these infections but do not show signs unless they are stressed. Symptoms include diarrhea, weight loss and lack of appetite. These infections are not always apparent in the fecal examination.

Whipworms are hard to find without a microscope, a job best left to a veterinarian. Pictured here are adult whipworms.

Tapeworms

Seldom apparent on fecal floatation, they are diagnosed frequently as rice-like segments around the dog's anus and the base of the tail. Tapeworms are long, flat and ribbon like, sometimes several feet in length, and made up of many segments about five-eighths of an inch long. The two most common types of tapeworms found in the dog are:

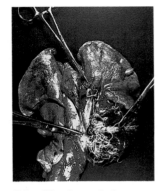

Dirofilaria—adult worms in a heart of a dog. Courtesy of Merck Ag Vet.

(1) First the larval form of the flea tapeworm parasite must mature in an intermediate host, the flea, before it can become infective. Your dog acquires this by ingesting the flea through licking and chewing.

(2) Rabbits, rodents and certain large game animals serve as intermediate hosts for other species of tapeworms. If your dog should eat one of these infected hosts, then he can acquire tapeworms.

HEARTWORM DISEASE

This is a worm that resides in the heart and adjacent blood vessels of the lung that produces microfilaria, which circulate in the bloodstream. It is possible for a dog to be infected with any number of worms from one to a hundred that can be 6 to 14 inches long. It is a life-threatening disease, expensive to treat and easily prevented. Depending on where you live, your veterinarian may recommend a preventive year-round and either an annual or semiannual blood test. The most common preventive is given once a month.

EXTERNAL PARASITES

Fleas

These pests are not only the dog's worst enemy but also enemy to the owner's pocketbook. Preventing is less expensive than treating, but regardless we'd prefer to spend our money elsewhere. Likely, the majority of our dogs are allergic to the bite of a flea, and in many cases it only takes one flea bite. The protein in the flea's saliva is the culprit. Allergic dogs have a reaction, which usually results in a "hot spot." More than likely such a reaction will involve a trip to the veterinarian for treatment. Yes, prevention is less expensive. Fortunately today there are several good products available.

If there is a flea infestation, no one product is going to correct the problem. Not only will the dog require treatment so will the environment. In general flea collars are not very effective although there is now available an "egg" collar that will kill the eggs on the dog. Dips are the most economical but they are messy. There are some effective shampoos and treatments available through pet shops and veterinarians. An oral tablet arrived on the American market in 1995 and was popular in Europe the previous year. It sterilizes the female flea but will not kill adult fleas. Therefore the tablet, which is given monthly, will decrease the flea population but is not a "cure-all." Those dogs that suffer from flea-bite allergy will still be subjected to the bite of the flea. Another popular parasiticide is permethrin, which is applied to the back of the dog in one or two places depending on the dog's weight. This product works as a repellent causing the flea to get "hot feet" and jump off. Do not confuse this product with some of the organophosphates that are also applied to the dog's back.

Some products are not usable on young puppies. Treating fleas should be done under your veterinarian's guidance. Frequently it is necessary to combine products and the layman does not have the knowledge regarding possible toxicities. It is hard to believe but there are a few dogs that do have a natural

resistance to fleas. Nevertheless it would be wise to treat all pets at the same time. Don't forget your cats. Cats just love to prowl the

The deer tick is the most common carrier of Lyme disease. Photo courtesy of Virbac Laboratories, Inc., Fort Worth, Texas.

The more time your Collie spends outside, the better chance he has of picking up parasites. Be sure to check your Collie's coat thoroughly for fleas and ticks.

neighborhood and consequently return with unwanted guests.

Adult fleas live on the dog but their eggs drop off the dog into the environment. There they go through four larval stages before reaching adulthood, and thereby are able to jump back on the poor unsuspecting dog. The cycle resumes and takes between 21 to 28 days under ideal conditions. There are environmental products available that will kill both the adult fleas and the larvae.

Ticks

Ticks carry Rocky Mountain Spotted Fever, Lyme disease and can cause tick paralysis. They should be removed with tweezers, trying to pull out the head. The jaws carry disease. There is a tick preventive collar that does an excellent job. The ticks automatically back out on those dogs wearing collars.

Sarcoptic Mange

This is a mite that is difficult to find on skin scrapings. The pinnal reflex is a good indicator of this disease. Rub the ends of the pinna (ear) together and the dog will start scratching with his foot. Sarcoptes are highly contagious to other dogs and to humans although they do not live long on humans. They cause intense itching.

Show your Collie you love him by providing him with the best possible health care for a long and fulfilling life.

Demodectic Mange

This is a mite that is passed from the dam to her puppies. It affects youngsters age three to ten months. Diagnosis is confirmed by skin scraping. Small areas of alopecia around the eyes, lips and/or forelegs become visible. There is little itching unless there is a secondary bacterial infection. Some breeds are afflicted more than others.

Cheyletiella

This causes intense itching and is diagnosed by skin scraping. It lives in the outer layers of the skin of dogs, cats, rabbits and humans. Yellow-gray scales may be found on the back and the rump, top of the head and the nose.

TO BREED OR NOT TO BREED

More than likely your breeder has requested that you have your puppy neutered or spayed. Your breeder's request is based on what is healthiest for your dog and what is most beneficial for your breed. Experienced and conscientious breeders devote many years into developing a bloodline. In order to do this, he makes every effort to plan each breeding in regard to conformation, temperament and health. This type of breeder does his best to perform the necessary testing (i.e.,

Your Collies eyes should be clear and free of any redness or irritation.

120

OFA, CERF, testing for inherited blood disorders, thyroid, etc.). Testing is expensive and sometimes very disheartening when a favorite dog doesn't pass his health tests. The health history pertains not only to the breeding stock but to the immediate ancestors. Reputable breeders do not want their offspring to be bred indiscriminately. Therefore you may be asked to neuter or spay your puppy. Of course there is always the exception, and your breeder may agree to let you breed your dog under his direct supervision. This is an important concept. More and more effort is being made to breed healthier dogs.

Spay/Neuter

There are numerous benefits of performing this surgery at six months of age. Unspayed females are subject to mammary and ovarian cancer. In order to prevent mammary cancer she must be spayed prior to her first heat cycle. Later in life, an unspayed female may develop a pyometra (an infected uterus), which is definitely life threatening.

Spaying is performed under a general anesthetic and is easy on the young dog. As you might expect it is a little harder on the older dog, but that is no reason to deny her the surgery. The surgery removes the ovaries and uterus. It is important to remove all the ovarian tissue. If some is left behind, she could remain attractive to males. In order to view the ovaries, a reasonably long incision is necessary. An ovariohysterectomy is considered major surgery.

Neutering the male at a young age will inhibit some characteristic male behavior that owners frown upon. Some boys will not hike their legs and mark territory if they are neutered at six months of age. Also neutering at a young age has hormonal benefits, lessening the chance of hormonal aggressiveness.

Surgery involves removing the testicles but leaving the scrotum. If there should be a retained testicle, then he definitely needs to be neutered before the age of two or three years. Retained testicles can develop into cancer. Unneutered males are at risk for testicular cancer, perineal fistulas, perianal tumors and fistulas and prostatic disease.

Intact males and females are prone to housebreaking accidents. Females urinate frequently before, during and after heat cycles, and males tend to mark territory if there is a female in heat. Males may show the same behavior if there is a visiting dog or guests.

Surgery involves a sterile operating procedure equivalent to human surgery. The incision site is shaved, surgically scrubbed and draped. The veterinarian wears a sterile surgical gown, cap, mask and gloves. Anesthesia should be monitored by a registered technician. It is customary for the veterinarian to recommend a pre-anesthetic blood screening, looking for metabolic problems and a ECG rhythm strip to check for normal heart function. Today anesthetics are equal to human anesthetics, which enables your dog to walk out of the clinic the same day as surgery.

Some folks worry about their dog gaining weight after being neutered or spayed. This is usually not the case. It is true that some dogs may be less active so they could develop a problem, but most dogs are just as active as they were before surgery. However, if your dog should begin to gain, then you need to decrease his food and see to it that he gets a little more exercise.

Genetic diseases can be passed from generation to generation. It is important to provide preventive health care and screenings to ensure healthy animals.

DENTAL CARE for Your Dog's Life

So you've got a new puppy! You also have a new set of puppy teeth in your household. Anyone who has ever raised a puppy is abundantly aware of these new teeth. Your puppy will chew anything it can reach, chase your shoelaces, and play "tear the rag" with any piece of clothing it can find. When puppies are newly born, they have no teeth. At about four weeks of age, puppies of most breeds begin to develop their deciduous or baby teeth. They begin eating semi-solid food, fighting and biting with their litter mates, and learning discipline from their mother. As their new teeth come in, they inflict more pain on their mother's breasts, so her feeding sessions become less frequent and shorter. By six or eight weeks, the mother will start growling to warn her pups when they are fighting too roughly or hurting her as they nurse too much with their new teeth.

Toys like the Plaque Attacker™ by Nylabone® help your Collie to combat plaque and tartar and are safe for aggressive chewers.

Puppies need to chew. It is a necessary part of their physical and mental development. They develop muscles and necessary life skills as they drag objects around, fight over possession, and vocalize alerts and warnings. Puppies chew on things to explore their world. They are using their sense of taste to determine what is food and what is not. How else can they tell an electrical cord from a lizard? At about four months of age, most puppies begin shedding their baby teeth. Often these teeth need some help to come out and make way for the permanent teeth. The incisors (front teeth) will be replaced first. Then, the adult canine or fang teeth erupt. When the baby tooth is not shed before the permanent tooth comes in, veterinarians call it a retained deciduous tooth. This condition will often cause gum infections by trapping hair and debris between the permanent tooth and the retained baby tooth. Nylafloss® is an excellent device for puppies to use. They can toss it, drag it, and chew on the many surfaces it presents. The baby teeth can catch in the nylon material, aiding in their

removal. Puppies that have adequate chew toys will have less destructive behavior, develop more physically, and have less chance of retained deciduous teeth.

During the first year, your dog should be seen by your veterinarian at regular intervals. Your veterinarian will let you know when to bring in your puppy for vaccinations and parasite examinations. At each visit, your veterinarian should inspect the lips, teeth, and mouth as part of a complete physical examination. You should take some part in the maintenance of your dog's oral health. You should examine your dog's mouth weekly throughout his first year to make sure there are no sores, foreign objects, tooth problems, etc. If your dog drools excessively, shakes its head, or has bad breath, consult your veterinarian. By the time your dog is six months old, the permanent teeth are all in and plaque can start to accumulate on the tooth surfaces. This is when your dog needs to develop good dental-care habits to prevent calculus build-up on its teeth. Brushing is best. That is a fact that cannot be denied. However, some dogs do not like their teeth brushed regularly, or you may not be able to accomplish the task. In that case, you should consider a product that will help prevent plaque and calculus build-up.

The Plaque Attackers® and Galileo Bone® are other excellent choices for the first three years of a dog's life. Their shapes make them interesting for the dog. As the dog chews on them, the solid polyurethane massages the gums which improves the blood circulation to the periodontal tissues. Projections on the chew devices increase the surface and are in contact with the

tooth for more efficient cleaning. The unique shape and consistency prevent your

Provide your Collie pup with plenty of Nylabones® to satisfy his desire to chew.

126

dog from exerting excessive force on his own teeth or from breaking off pieces of the bone. If your dog is an aggressive chewer or weighs more than 55 pounds (25 kg), you should consider giving him a Nylabone®, the most durable chew product on the market.

As a pet owner, it is essential to keep your dog's teeth clean. The 2-Brush™ by Nylabone® is made with two toothbrushes to clean both sides of your dog's teeth at the same time.

The Gumabones ®, made by the Nylabone Company, is constructed of strong polyurethane, which is softer than nylon. Less powerful chewers prefer

A thorough oral examination should be a part of your Collie's regular veterinary check-up.

the Gumabones® to the Nylabones®. A super option for your dog is the Hercules Bone®, a uniquely shaped bone named after the great Olympian for its exception strength. Like all Nylabone products, they are specially scented to make them attractive to your dog. Ask your veterinarian about these bones and he will validate the good doctor's prescription: Nylabones® not only give your dog a good chewing workout but also help to save your dog's teeth (and even his life, as it protects him from possible fatal periodontal diseases).

By the time dogs are four years old, 75% of them have periodontal disease. It is the most common infection in dogs. Yearly examinations by your veterinarian are essential to maintaining your dog's good health. If your veterinarian detects periodontal disease, he or she may recommend a prophylactic cleaning. To do a thorough cleaning, it will be

The Hercules™ is made of very tough polyurethane and the raised dental tips massage the gums and remove the plaque from your dog's teeth.

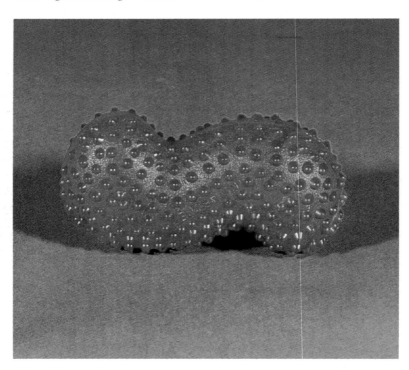

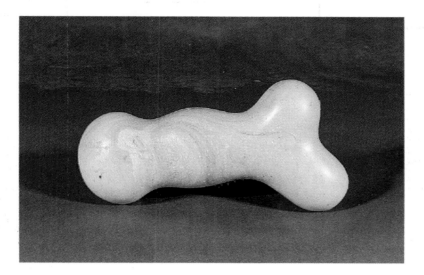

necessary to put your dog under anesthesia. With modern gas anesthetics and monitoring equipment, the procedure is pretty safe. Your veterinarian will scale the teeth with an ultrasound scaler or hand instrument. This removes the calculus from the teeth. If there are calculus deposits below the gum line, the veterinarian will plane the roots to make them smooth. After all of the calculus has been removed, the teeth are polished with pumice in a polishing cup. If any medical or surgical treatment is needed, it is done at this time. The final step would be fluoride treatment and your follow-up treatment at home. If the periodontal disease is advanced, the veterinarian may prescribe a medicated mouth rinse or antibiotics for use at home. Make sure your dog has safe, clean and attractive chew toys and treats. Chooz® treats are another way of using a consumable treat to help keep your dog's teeth clean.

Rawhide is the most popular of all materials for a dog to chew. This has never been good news to dog owners, because rawhide is inherently very dangerous for dogs. Thousands of dogs have died from rawhide, having swallowed the hide after it has become soft and mushy, only to cause stomach and intestinal blockage. A new rawhide product on the market has finally solved the problem of rawhide: molded Roar-Hide® from Nylabone. These are composed of processed, cut up, and melted American rawhide injected into your dog's favorite shape: a dog bone. These dog-safe devices smell and taste like rawhide but don't break up. The ridges on the bones help to fight tartar build-up on the teeth and they last ten times longer than the usual rawhide chews.

The Nylabone® Frisbee™ is a must if you want to have fun with your Collie and provide him with plenty of exercise.
The trademark Frisbee is used under license from Mattel, Inc., California, USA.

As your dog ages, professional examination and cleaning should become more frequent. The mouth should be inspected at least once a year. Your veterinarian may recommend visits every six months. In the geriatric patient, organs such as the heart, liver, and kidneys do not function as well as when they were young. Your veterinarian will probably want to test these organs' functions prior to using general anesthesia for dental cleaning. If your dog is a good chewer and you work closely with your veterinarian, your dog can keep all of its teeth all of its life. However, as your dog ages, his sense of smell, sight, and taste will diminish. He may not have the desire to chase, trap or chew his toys. He will also not have the energy to chew for long periods, as arthritis and periodontal disease make chewing painful. This will leave you with more responsibility for keeping his teeth clean and healthy. The dog that would not let you brush his teeth at one year of age, may let you brush his teeth now that he is ten years old.

If you train your dog with good chewing habits as a puppy, he will have healthier teeth throughout his life.

Give your Collie a Nylafloss™ to play with. Not only does it provide hours of fun for your dog, it literally flosses his teeth while he chews.

TRAVELING with Your Collie

T he earlier you start traveling with your new puppy or dog, the better. He needs to become accustomed to traveling. However, some dogs are nervous riders and become carsick easily. It is helpful if he starts with an empty stomach. Do not despair, as it will go better if you continue taking him with you on short fun rides. How would you feel if every time you rode in the car you stopped at the doctor's for an injection? You would soon dread that nasty car. Older dogs that tend to get carsick may have more of a problem adjusting to traveling. Those dogs that are having a serious problem may benefit from some medication prescribed by the veterinarian.

Do give your dog a chance to relieve himself before getting into the car. It is a good idea to be prepared for a clean up with a leash, paper towels, bag and terry cloth towel.

The earlier you start traveling with your Collie, the sooner he will become accustomed to car rides.

The safest place for your dog is in a fiberglass crate, although close confinement can promote carsickness in some dogs. If your dog is nervous you can try letting him ride on the seat next to you or in someone's lap.

An alternative to the crate would be to use a car harness made for dogs and/or a safety strap attached to the harness or collar. Whatever you do, do not let your dog ride in the back of a pickup truck unless he is securely tied on a very short lead. I've seen trucks stop quickly and, even though the dog was tied, it fell out and was dragged.

Another advantage of the crate is that it is a safe place to leave him if you need to run into the store. Otherwise you

A well-trained Collie can accompany you anywhere. Ch. Sunnymede Deacon Blues owned by Diane Kissal doesn't want to be left behind!

wouldn't be able to leave the windows down. Keep in mind that while many dogs are overly protective in their crates, this may not be enough to deter dognappers. In some states it is against the law to leave a dog in the car unattended.

Never leave a dog loose in the car wearing a collar and leash. More than one dog has killed himself by hanging. Do not let him put his head out an open window. Foreign debris can be blown into his eyes. When leaving your dog unattended in a car, consider the temperature. It can take less than five minutes to reach temperatures over 100 degrees Fahrenheit.

TRIPS

Perhaps you are taking a trip. Give consideration to what is best for your dog—traveling with you or boarding. When

traveling by car, van or motor home, you need to think ahead about locking your vehicle. In all probability you have many valuables in the car and do not wish to leave it unlocked. Perhaps most valuable and not replaceable is your dog. Give thought to securing your vehicle and providing adequate ventilation for him. Another consideration for you when traveling with your dog is medical problems that may arise and little inconveniences, such as exposure to external parasites. Some areas of the country are quite flea infested. You may want to carry flea spray with you. This is even a good idea when staying in motels. Quite possibly you are not the only occupant of the room.

If you must leave your Collie behind for a short period of time, make sure he is in a secure fenced-in area.

Unbelievably many motels and even hotels do allow canine guests, even some very first-class ones. Gaines Pet Foods Corporation publishes *Touring With Towser*, a directory of domestic hotels and motels that accommodate guests with dogs. Their address is Gaines TWT, PO Box 5700, Kankakee, IL, 60902. Call ahead to any motel that you may be considering and see if they accept pets. Sometimes it is necessary to pay a deposit against room damage. The management may feel reassured if you mention that your dog will be crated. If you do travel with your dog, take along plenty of baggies so that you can clean up after him. When we all do our share in cleaning up, we make it possible for motels to continue accepting our pets. As a matter of fact, you should practice cleaning up everywhere you take your dog.

Depending on where your are traveling, you may need an up-to-date health certificate issued by your veterinarian. It is good policy to take along your dog's medical information, which would include the name, address and phone number of your veterinarian, vaccination record, rabies certificate, and any medication he is taking.

If you take your Collie with you on vacation, bring along a few of his things to make him feel more comfortable.

AIR TRAVEL

When traveling by air, you need to contact the airlines to check their policy. Usually you have to make arrangements up to a couple of weeks in advance for traveling with your dog. The airlines require your dog to travel in an airline approved fiberglass crate. Usually these can be purchased through the airlines but they are also readily available in most pet-supply stores. If your dog is not accustomed to a crate, then it is a good idea to get him acclimated to it before your trip. The day of the actual trip you should withhold water about one hour ahead of departure and no food for about 12 hours. The airlines generally have temperature restrictions, which do not allow pets to travel if it is either too cold or too hot. Frequently these restrictions are based on the temperatures at the departure and arrival airports. It's best to inquire about a health certificate. These usually need to be issued within ten days of departure. You should arrange for non-stop, direct flights and if a commuter plane should be involved, check to see if it will carry dogs. Some don't. The Humane Society of the United

Collies are so easygoing that they can make themselves at home almost anywhere.

Your Collie must get used to extensive traveling if he is to compete in dog shows.

States has put together a tip sheet for airline traveling. You can receive a copy by sending a self-addressed stamped envelope to:

The Humane Society of the United States
Tip Sheet
2100 L Street NW
Washington, DC 20037.

Regulations differ for traveling outside of the country and are sometimes changed without notice. Well in advance you need to write or call the appropriate consulate or agricultural department for instructions. Some countries have lengthy quarantines (six months), and countries differ in their rabies vaccination requirements. For instance, it may have to be given at least 30 days ahead of your departure.

Do make sure your dog is wearing proper identification including your name, phone number and city. You never know when you might be in an accident and separated from your dog. Or your dog could be frightened and somehow manage to escape and run away.

Another suggestion would be to carry in-case-of-emergency instructions. These would include the address and phone number of a relative or friend, your veterinarian's name, address and phone number, and your dog's medical information.

Whether lounging at home or roughing it in the wild, the Collie is a very adaptable dog and can adjust to any situation.

BOARDING KENNELS

Perhaps you have decided that you need to board your dog. Your veterinarian can recommend a good boarding facility or possibly a pet sitter that will come to your house. It is customary for the boarding kennel to ask for proof of vaccination for the DHLPP, rabies and bordetella vaccine. The bordetella should have been given within six months of boarding. This is for your protection. If they do not ask for this proof I would not board at their kennel. Ask about flea control. Those dogs that suffer flea-bite allergy can get in trouble at a boarding kennel. Unfortunately boarding kennels are limited on how much they are able to do.

For more information on pet sitting, contact NAPPS:
National Association of Professional Pet Sitters
1200 G Street, NW
Suite 760
Washington, DC 20005.

Some pet clinics have technicians that pet sit and technicians that board clinic patients in their homes. This may be an alternative for you. Ask your veterinarian if they have an employee that can help you. There is a definite advantage of having a technician care for your dog, especially if your dog is on medication or is a senior citizen.

You can write for a copy of *Traveling With Your Pet* from ASPCA, Education Department, 441 E. 92nd Street, New York, NY 10128.

A reputable boarding kennel will require that dogs receive the vaccination for kennel cough no less than two weeks before their scheduled stay.

IDENTIFICATION and Finding the Lost Dog

There are several ways of identifying your dog. The old standby is a collar with dog license, rabies, and ID tags. Unfortunately collars have a way of being separated from the dog and tags fall off. We're not suggesting you shouldn't use a collar and tags. If they stay intact and on the dog, they are the quickest way of identification.

For several years owners have been tattooing their dogs. Some tattoos use a number with a registry. Here lies the problem because there are several registries to check. If you wish to tattoo, use your social security number. The humane shelters have the means to trace it. It is usually done on the inside of the rear thigh. The area is first shaved and numbed. There is no pain, although a few dogs do not like the buzzing sound. Occasionally tattooing is not legible and needs to be redone.

The newest method of identification is microchipping. The microchip is a computer chip that is no larger than a grain of rice. The veterinarian implants it by injection between the shoulder blades. The dog feels no discomfort. If your dog is lost and picked up by the humane society, they can trace you by scanning the microchip, which has its own code. Microchip scanners are friendly to other brands of microchips and their registries. The microchip comes with a dog tag saying the dog is microchipped. It is the safest way of identifying your dog.

FINDING THE LOST DOG

I am sure you will agree that there would be little worse than losing your dog. Responsible pet owners rarely lose their dogs. They do not let their dogs run free because they don't want harm to come to them. Not only that but in most, if not all, states there is a leash law.

Beware of fenced-in yards. They can be a hazard. Dogs find ways to escape either over or under the fence. Another fast exit is through the gate that perhaps the neighbor's child left unlocked.

Below is a list that hopefully will be of help to you if you need it. Remember don't give up, keep looking. Your dog is worth your efforts.

1. Contact your neighbors and put flyers with a photo on it in their mailboxes. Information you should include would be the dog's name, breed, sex, color, age, source of identification, when your dog was last seen and where, and your name and phone numbers. It may be helpful to say the dog needs medical care. Offer a *reward*.

Leave your Collie in a safe, secure area when outside and off lead. This trio of Smooth Collies enjoys some time in the snow.

2. Check all local shelters daily. It is also possible for your dog to be picked up away from home and end up in an out-of-the-way shelter. Check these too. Go in person. It is not good enough to call. Most shelters are limited on the time they can hold dogs then they are put up for adoption or euthanized. There is the possibility that your dog will not make it to the shelter for several days. Your dog could have been wandering or someone may have tried to keep him.

3. Notify all local veterinarians. Call and send flyers.

4. Call your breeder. Frequently breeders are contacted when one of their breed is found.

5. Contact the rescue group for your breed.

6. Contact local schools—children may have seen your dog.

7. Post flyers at the schools, groceries, gas stations, convenience stores, veterinary clinics, groomers and any other place that will allow them.

8. Advertise in the newspaper.

9. Advertise on the radio.

BEHAVIOR and Canine Communication

Studies of the human/animal bond point out the importance of the unique relationships that exist between people and their pets. Those of us who share our lives with pets understand the special part they play through companionship, service and protection. For many, the pet/owner bond goes beyond simple companionship; pets are often considered members of the family. A leading pet food manufacturer recently conducted a nationwide survey of pet owners to gauge just how important pets were in their lives. Here's what they found:

- 76 percent allow their pets to sleep on their beds
- 78 percent think of their pets as their children
- 84 percent display photos of their pets, mostly in their homes

It has been found that spending time with a dog can reduce stress and improve your quality of life. Who could help but smile at a cute Collie puppy?

- 84 percent think that their pets react to their own emotions
- 100 percent talk to their pets
- 97 percent think that their pets understand what they're saying

Are you surprised?

Senior citizens show more concern for their own eating habits when they have the responsibility of feeding a dog. Seeing that their dog is routinely exercised encourages the owner to think of schedules that otherwise may seem

unimportant to the senior citizen. The older owner may be arthritic and feeling poorly

The bond between the Collie and his owner is a strong one.

but with responsibility for his dog he has a reason to get up and get moving. It is a big plus if his dog is an attention seeker who will demand such from his owner.

Over the last couple of decades, it has been shown that pets relieve the stress of those who lead busy lives. Owning a pet has been known to lessen the occurrence of heart attack and stroke.

Many single folks thrive on the companionship of a dog. Lifestyles are very different from a long time ago, and today more individuals seek the single life. However, they receive fulfillment from owning a dog.

Most likely the majority of our dogs live in family environments. The companionship they provide is well worth the effort involved. In my opinion, every child should have the opportunity to have a family dog. Dogs teach responsibility through understanding their care, feelings and even respecting their life cycles. Frequently those children who have not been exposed to dogs grow up afraid of dogs, which isn't good. Dogs sense timidity and some will take advantage of the situation.

Today more dogs are serving as service dogs. Since the origination of the Seeing Eye dogs years ago, we now have trained hearing dogs. Also dogs are trained to provide service for the handicapped and are able to perform many different tasks for their owners. Search and Rescue dogs, with their handlers, are sent throughout the world to assist in recovery of disaster victims. They are life savers.

A positive relationship with his dam and littermates is the first step to a well-socialized Collie.

Therapy dogs are very popular with nursing homes, and some hospitals even allow them to visit. The inhabitants truly look forward to their visits. They wanted and were allowed to have visiting dogs in their beds to hold and love.

Nationally there is a Pet Awareness Week to educate students and others about the value and basic care of our pets. Many countries take an even greater interest in their pets than Americans do. In those countries the pets are allowed to accompany their owners into restaurants and shops, etc. In the U.S. this freedom is only available

Children make great playmates for the energetic Collie—and vice versa!

A loyal and affectionate dog like the Collie will thrive when allowed to be a member of the family. Katie owned by Mary Cox snoozes in her favorite spot.

to our service dogs. Even so we think very highly of the human/animal bond.

CANINE BEHAVIOR

Canine behavior problems are the number-one reason for pet owners to dispose of their dogs, either through new homes, humane shelters or euthanasia. Unfortunately there are too many owners who are unwilling to devote the necessary time to properly train their dogs. On the other hand, there are those who not only are concerned about inherited health problems but are also aware of the dog's mental stability.

You may realize that a breed and his group relatives (i.e., sporting, hounds, etc.) show tendencies to behavioral characteristics. An experienced breeder can acquaint you with his breed's personality. Unfortunately many breeds are labeled with poor temperaments when actually the breed as a whole is not affected but only a small percentage of individuals within the breed.

Even the most even-tempered Collie can develop behavior problems, which is why it is important to be a firm and fair owner.

Inheritance and environment contribute to the dog's behavior. Some naïve people suggest inbreeding as the cause of bad temperaments. Inbreeding only results in poor behavior if the ancestors carry the trait. If there are excellent temperaments behind the dogs, then inbreeding will promote good temperaments in the offspring. Did you ever consider that inbreeding is what sets the characteristics of a breed? A purebred dog is the end result of inbreeding. This does not spare the mixed-breed dog from the same problems. Mixed-breed dogs frequently are the offspring of purebred dogs.

Not too many decades ago most of our dogs led a different lifestyle than what is prevalent today. Usually mom stayed home so the dog had human companionship and someone to discipline it if needed. Not much was expected from the dog. Today's mom works and everyone's life is at a much faster pace.

Dogs love to eat "people food" but should not be allowed to grab or beg. Good manners are an important trait for your Collie to possess.

The dog may have to adjust to being a "weekend" dog. The family is gone all day during the week, and the dog is left to his own devices for entertainment. Some dogs sleep all day waiting for their family to come home and others become wigwam wreckers if given the opportunity. Crates do ensure the safety of the dog and the house. However, he could become a physically and emotionally cripple if he doesn't get enough exercise and attention. We still appreciate and want

the companionship of our dogs although we expect more from them. In many cases we tend to forget dogs are just that— *dogs* not human beings.

SOCIALIZING AND TRAINING

Puppies have no trouble getting into mischief! Your Collie must always know who is the boss in your relationship.

Many prospective puppy buyers lack experience regarding the proper socialization and training needed to develop the type of pet we all desire. In the first 18 months, training does take some work. It is easier to start proper training before there is a problem that needs to be corrected.

The initial work begins with the breeder. The breeder should start socializing the puppy at five to six weeks of age and cannot let up. Human socializing is critical up through 12 weeks of age and likewise important during the following months. The litter should be left together during the first few weeks but it is necessary to separate them by ten weeks of age. Leaving them together after that time will increase competition for litter dominance. If puppies are not socialized with people by 12 weeks of age, they will be timid in later life.

The eight- to ten-week age period is a fearful time for puppies. They need to be handled very gently around children and adults. There should be no harsh discipline during this time. Starting at 14 weeks of age, the puppy begins the juvenile period, which ends when he reaches sexual maturity around six to 14 months of age. During the juvenile period he needs to be introduced to strangers (adults, children and other dogs) on the home property. At sexual maturity he will begin to bark at strangers and become more protective. Males start to lift their legs to urinate but if you desire you can inhibit this behavior by walking your boy on leash away from trees, shrubs, fences, etc.

Taking responsibility for a dog can give a person a purpose in life. Of course, playing with an adorable Collie puppy can brighten anyone's day.

Perhaps you are thinking about an older puppy. You need to inquire about the

The athletic Collie needs plenty of play and exercise, not only to combat boredom, but also for his general well being.

puppy's social experience. If he has lived in a kennel, he may have a hard time adjusting to people and environmental stimuli. Assuming he has had a good social upbringing, there are advantages to an older puppy.

Training includes puppy kindergarten and a minimum of one to two basic training classes. During these classes you will learn how to dominate your youngster. This is especially important if you own a large breed of dog. It is somewhat harder, if not nearly impossible, for some owners to be the Alpha figure when their dog towers over them. You will be taught how to properly restrain your dog. This concept is important. Again it puts you in the Alpha position. All dogs need to be restrained many times during their lives. Believe it or not, some of our worst offenders are the eight-week-old puppies that are brought to our clinic. They need to be gently restrained for a nail trim but the way they carry on you would think we were killing them. In comparison, their vaccination is a "piece of cake." When we ask dogs to do something that is not agreeable to them, then their worst comes out. Life will be easier for your dog if you expose him at a young age to the necessities of life–proper behavior and restraint.

UNDERSTANDING THE DOG'S LANGUAGE

Most authorities agree that the dog is a descendent of the wolf. The dog and wolf have similar traits. For instance both are pack oriented and prefer not to be isolated for long periods of time. Another characteristic is that the dog, like the wolf, looks to the leader–Alpha–for direction. Both the wolf and the dog communicate through body language, not only within their pack but with outsiders.

Curb your Collie's tendency to chew by providing him with plenty of Nylabones®. Your Collie and your furniture will thank you for it!

Every pack has an Alpha figure. The dog looks to you, or should look to you, to be that leader. If your dog doesn't receive the proper training and guidance, he very well may replace you as Alpha. This would be a serious problem and is certainly a disservice to your dog.

Eye contact is one way the Alpha wolf keeps order within his pack. You are Alpha so you must establish eye contact with your puppy. Obviously your puppy will have to look at you. Practice eye contact even if you need to hold his head for five to ten seconds at a time. You can give him a treat as a reward. Make sure your eye contact is gentle and not threatening. Later, if he has been naughty, it is permissible to give him a long, penetrating look. There are some older dogs that never learned eye contact as puppies and cannot accept eye contact. You should avoid eye contact with these dogs since they feel threatened and will retaliate as such.

151

BODY LANGUAGE

The play bow, when the forequarters are down and the hindquarters are elevated, is an invitation to play. Puppies play fight, which helps them learn the acceptable limits of biting. This is necessary for later in their lives. Nevertheless, an owner may be falsely reassured by the playful nature of his dog's aggression. Playful aggression toward another dog or human may be an indication of serious aggression in the future. Owners should never play fight or play tug-of-war with any dog that is inclined to be dominant.

Signs of submission are:

1. Avoids eye contact.
2. Active submission—the dog crouches down, ears back and the tail is lowered.
3. Passive submission—the dog rolls on his side with his hindlegs in the air and frequently urinates.

Signs of dominance are:

1. Makes eye contact.
2. Stands with ears up, tail up and the hair raised on his neck.
3. Shows dominance over another dog by standing at right angles over it.

Dominant dogs tend to behave in characteristic ways such as:

1. The dog may be unwilling to move from

A dominant pup's personality will be evident in the way he interacts with his littermates. This type of dog will need a firm owner.

If your Collie pup displays some timidness, respect his feelings and give him time to become used to the situation.

his place (i.e., reluctant to give up the sofa if the owner wants to sit there).

2. He may not part with toys or objects in his mouth and may show possessiveness with his food bowl.

3. He may not respond quickly to commands.

4. He may be disagreeable for grooming and dislikes to be petted.

Dogs are popular because of their sociable nature. Those that have contact with humans during the first 12 weeks of life regard them as a member of their own species—their pack. All dogs have the potential for both dominant and submissive behavior. Only through experience and training do they learn to whom it is appropriate to show which behavior. Not all dogs are concerned with dominance but owners need to be aware of that potential. It is wise for the owner to establish his dominance early on.

A human can express dominance or submission toward a dog in the following ways:

1. Meeting the dog's gaze signals dominance. Averting the gaze signals submission. If the dog growls or threatens, averting the gaze is the first avoiding action to take—it may prevent attack. It is important to establish eye contact in the puppy. The older dog that has not been exposed to

153

eye contact may see it as a threat and will not be willing to submit.

2. Being taller than the dog signals dominance; being lower signals submission. This is why, when attempting to make friends with a strange dog or catch the runaway, one should kneel down to his level. Some owners see their dogs become dominant when allowed on the furniture or on the bed. Then he is at the owner's level.

3. An owner can gain dominance by ignoring all the dog's social initiatives. The owner pays attention to the dog only when he obeys a command.

No dog should be allowed to achieve dominant status over any adult or child. Ways of preventing are as follows:

1. Handle the puppy gently, especially during the three- to four-month period.

2. Let the children and adults handfeed him and teach him to take food without lunging or grabbing.

3. Do not allow him to chase children or joggers.

4. Do not allow him to jump on people or mount their legs. Even females may be inclined to mount. It is not only a male habit.

5. Do not allow him to growl for any reason.

6. Don't participate in wrestling or tug-of-war games.

7. Don't physically punish puppies for aggressive behavior. Restrain him from repeating the infraction and teach an alternative behavior. Dogs should earn everything they receive from their owners. This would include sitting to receive petting or treats, sitting before going out the door and sitting to receive the collar and leash. These types of exercises reinforce the owner's dominance.

Young children should never be left alone with a dog. It is important that children learn some basic obedience commands so they have some control over the dog. They will gain the respect of their dog.

FEAR

One of the most common problems dogs experience is being fearful. Some dogs are more afraid than others. On the lesser side, which is sometimes humorous to watch, dogs can be afraid of a strange object. They act silly when something is out of place in the house. We call his problem perceptive intelligence. He realizes the abnormal within his known environment. He does not react the same way in strange environments since he does not know what is normal.

On the more serious side is a fear of people. This can result in backing off, seeking his own space and saying "leave me alone" or it can result in an aggressive behavior that may lead to challenging the person. Respect that the dog wants to be left alone and give him time to come forward. If you approach the cornered dog, he may resort to snapping. If you leave him alone, he may decide to come forward, which should be rewarded with a treat.

Collies should be able to play together without displaying any fear, dominance, or aggression.

Some dogs may initially be too fearful to take treats. In these cases it is helpful to make sure the dog hasn't eaten for about 24 hours. Being a little hungry encourages him to accept the treats, especially if they are of the "gourmet"

variety.

Dogs can be afraid of numerous things, including loud noises and thunderstorms. Invariably the owner rewards (by comforting) the dog when it shows signs of fearfulness. When your dog is frightened, direct his attention to something else and act happy. Don't dwell on his fright.

AGGRESSION

Some different types of aggression are: predatory, defensive, dominance, possessive, protective, fear induced, noise provoked, "rage" syndrome (unprovoked aggression), maternal and aggression directed toward other dogs. Aggression is the most common behavioral problem encountered. Protective breeds are expected to be more aggressive than others but with the proper upbringing they can make very dependable companions. You need to be able to read your dog.

Many factors contribute to aggression including genetics and environment. An improper environment, which may include the living conditions, lack of social life, excessive punishment, being attacked or frightened by an aggressive dog, etc., can all influence a dog's behavior. Even spoiling him and giving too much praise may be detrimental. Isolation and the lack of human contact or exposure to frequent teasing by children or adults also can ruin a good dog.

Lack of direction, fear, or confusion lead to aggression in those dogs that are so inclined. Any obedience exercise, even the sit and down, can direct the dog and overcome fear and/or confusion. Every dog should learn these commands as a youngster, and there should be periodic reinforcement.

When a dog is showing signs of aggression, you should speak calmly (no screaming or hysterics) and firmly give a command that he understands, such as the sit. As soon as your dog obeys, you have assumed your dominant position. Aggression presents a problem because there may be danger to others. Sometimes it is an emotional issue. Owners may consciously or unconsciously encourage their dog's aggression. Other owners show responsibility by accepting the problem and taking measures to keep it under control. The owner is responsible for his dog's actions, and it is not wise to take a chance on someone being bitten, especially a child. Euthanasia is the solution for some owners and in severe cases this may be the best choice. However, few dogs are that dangerous and very few are that much of a threat to their owners. If caution is exercised and professional help is gained early on, most cases can be controlled.

Some authorities recommend feeding a lower protein (less than 20 percent) diet. They believe this can aid in reducing aggression. If the dog loses weight, then vegetable oil can be added. Veterinarians and behaviorists are having some success with pharmacology. In many cases treatment is possible and can improve the situation.

Body language and expression can reveal a lot of what your Collie is thinking. Happiness is written all over this Collie smile!

If you have done everything according to "the book" regarding training and socializing and are still having a behavior problem, don't procrastinate. It is important that the problem gets attention before it is out of hand. It is estimated that 20 percent of a veterinarian's time may be devoted to dealing with problems before they become so intolerable that the dog is separated from its home and owner. If your veterinarian isn't able to help, he should refer you to a behaviorist.

PROBLEMS

Barking

This is a habit that shouldn't be encouraged. Some owners desire their dog to bark so as to be a watchdog. Most dogs will bark when a stranger comes to the door.

The new puppy frequently barks or whines in the crate in his strange environment and the owner reinforces the puppy's bad behavior by going to him during the night. This is a no-no. Smack the top of the crate and say "quiet" in a loud, firm voice. The puppies don't like to hear the loud noise of the crate being banged. If the barking is sleep-interrupting, then the owner should take crate and pup to the bedroom for a few days until the puppy becomes adjusted to his new environment. Otherwise ignore the barking during the night.

Barking can be an inherited problem or a bad habit learned through the environment. It takes dedication to stop the barking. Attention should be paid to the cause of the barking. Does the dog seek attention, does he need to go out, is it feeding time, is it occurring when he is left alone, is it a protective bark, etc.? Overzealous barking is an inherited tendency. When barking presents a problem for you, try to stop it as soon as it begins.

There are electronic collars available that are supposed to curb barking. There are some disadvantages to to the collar. If the dog is barking out of excitement, punishment is not the appropriate treatment. Presumably there is the chance the collar could be activated by other stimuli and thereby punish the dog when it is not barking. Should you decide to use one, then you should seek help from a person with experience with that type of collar. Nevertheless the root of the problem needs to be investigated and corrected.

In extreme circumstances (usually when there is a problem with the neighbors), some people have resorted to having their dogs debarked. I caution you that the dog continues to bark

but usually only a squeaking sound is heard. Frequently the vocal cords grow back. Probably the biggest concern is that the dog can be left with scar tissue which can narrow the opening to the trachea.

Many people thrive on the devoted companionship that a Collie can provide.

SUGGESTED READING

PS-825
The Collie
320 pages.

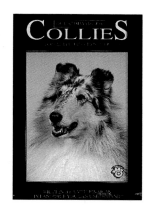

BB-109
Dr. Ackerman's Book of Collies
96 pages, 75 full-color photos.

RE-306
Guide to Owning a Collie
65 pages, 50 full-color photos.

TS-257
Choosing a Dog for Life
384 pages, over 700 full-color photos.

INDEX